Encyclopedia of Animation Techniques

Encyclopedia of Animation Techniques

Richard Taylor

CHARTWELL
BOOKS, INC.

A QUARTO BOOK

This edition published in 2003 by
Chartwell Books
A division of Book Sales, Inc.
114 Northfield Avenue
Edison, New Jersey 08837
USA

Copyright © 1996, 2003 Quarto Publishing plc

This book was designed and produced by
Quarto Publishing
The Old Brewery
6 Blundell Street
London N7 9BH

ISBN 0-7858-1805-7

QUAR.TOA

Designer Graham Davis
Senior editor Kate Kirby
Copy editor Hazel Harrison
Senior art editor Elizabeth Healey
Picture researcher Guilia Hetherington
Photographers Paul Forrester, Colin Bowling, Martin Norris
Animators Beverly Knowlden (model); Dick Taylor (cut-out);
Ronaldo Canfora, Roy Elsworth, Mike Adams (drawn); Stephen
Marjoram (computer)
Technical illustrators Gary Cross, Graham White, Dave Kemp
Editorial director Mark Dartford
Art director Moira Clinch

Typeset in Great Britain by Central Southern Typesetters,
Eastbourne
Manufactured in Malyasia by CH Colour Scan Sdn. Bhd
Printed in China

A Close Shave by Nick Park at
Aardman Animation. Wallace
meets Wendolene, "Their
hands touch for the first time."

Contents

Introduction

◄▼ *Betty Boop*, Fleischer Brothers, drawn by Grim Natwick. *Felix the Cat*, Pat Sullivan Productions, drawn by Otto Messmer. Images from the springtime of animation in the 1920s. Techniques and styles may have become more varied and sophisticated, but the zest and boldness of these films has never been surpassed.

▲ *West and Soda*, Bruno Bozzetto. From the fertile period of the 1960s when the careful naturalism of the '30s and '40s had given way to the more astringent styles initiated at UPA. Stylistically, the image acknowledges the influence of 20th-century painting. In creative spirit the films were sharper observers of human behavior. This is a European film. It is in Europe that experiment has been enthusiastically pursued.

Animation is normally defined as the creation of an illusion of movement by assembling a sequence of still images. Before going on to describe techniques of animation, it is important to emphasize that the quality of the sequence is more important than the quality of the images. It is possible to make a bad film with beautiful drawings or models—the art of animated film is in the action.

Animation consists of imagining and representing action. Think of the events you wish to portray, then find the means to represent them. Of course, each creator's vision will guide the sort of image which is used to convey the action, but it is the sequence of events which is the primary matter to be conveyed to the viewer. The nature of the image is the means of conveying that matter.

Animation is not making drawings move. It is, in essence, drawing movement. Some years ago, Norman McLaren made the same statement in his book *On the Creative Process* (edited by Donald McWilliam, National Film Board of Canada). He went on to say, "How it moves is more important than what moves. Though what moves is important, in relative order of importance, it's how it moves that's the important thing . . . What the animator does on each frame of film is not as important as what he or she does in between."

From these ringing statements, it can be seen that using the form of a book to describe animation techniques is starting at a disadvantage. It is possible to use only still images as illustration, and the "what happens in between" can get little or no visual demonstration—merely written explanations.

Unlike many art and craft techniques, no animation technique in itself produces a complete object. Instead, each one contributes to a whole, which is the completed film. Story structure, storyboarding, design, the various drawing techniques, model making, the paramount skills of movement and timing, filming, soundtracks, and editing are all techniques in themselves, and in most professional productions, each is practiced by a specialized craftsman. Comprehending and coordinating these techniques is the job of the director. There is no way of describing the "technique" of direction, although some of the tools used in direction will be referred to.

The making of animated film requires a large volume of work and technical processes of some complexity. Because of this, animation production has been influenced by industrial methods of production, and this is the origin of the separation of crafts referred to.

Although I personally believe that the best animation is produced by a team, unified in spirit and intention, it is possible for

▼ *Strings*, Wendy Tilby, National Film Board of Canada. A film from Canada where, in the National Film Board, a great nursery of adventure and experiment in animation was established. This 1980s film, animated by progressive painting on glass, typifies how a variety of techniques was explored at the Film Board as well as in Europe.

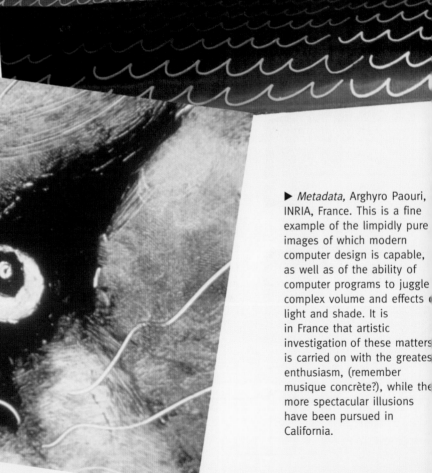

▶ *Metadata,* Arghyro Paouri, INRIA, France. This is a fine example of the limpidly pure images of which modern computer design is capable, as well as of the ability of computer programs to juggle complex volume and effects of light and shade. It is in France that artistic investigation of these matters is carried on with the greatest enthusiasm, (remember musique concrète?), while the more spectacular illusions have been pursued in California.

◀ *Screenplay*, Barry Purves, Bare Boards Productions. Made in the 1990s, this bears evidence to the recent vigor of British animation. Many of the animators and designers were able to develop their skills on expensively funded advertising, and the finesse and polish of design and puppet making, as well as the split-second timing which characterizes Barry Purves' work, are typical of those who learned their trade in commercials.

one person or a very small group to create a complete film. As far as possible, this book places emphasis on techniques which are suitable for those with limited resources.

To be involved in a book on animation techniques at this particular time might be compared to describing the river bank while traveling in a canoe over the rapid. At no time in the past has the technology which relates to the making of images been in such a rapid process of change. It would be impossible to give a detailed assessment of each development, since every day seems to bring a new one. We have thus concentrated on traditional processes, none of which are yet obsolete nor ever likely to perish, just as the sampler and the electronic keyboard have not caused every violin, guitar, and trumpet to be destroyed. Moreover, traditional methods are a rational choice for certain of the qualities they retain, as well as being accessible at comparatively low cost for those making their first experiments in animation. The basic ingredients of animated film—storytelling, design, and control of movement—are not machine products, but those of imagination and intelligence. The computer can help to execute the work, but the work itself must be conceived and designed by experienced brains and hands.

It should always be remembered that an animated film is a piece of industrial design fashioned for a purpose, which in this case is to communicate. There are three functions of animated films: to entertain, to educate, or to inform. The term "entertain" should be taken to include everything from farce to tragedy, as well as those works which, less dramatic in intention, are nevertheless designed to move the viewer. Just as the external form of an aircraft is the product of the engineering which allows it to fly, the finished form of an animated film is governed by the considerations which enable it to communicate. No airplane would get off the ground if it were designed simply to look pretty, and, similarly, to think only of the appeal of the drawings or puppets without regard to the way they are used is to misunderstand the medium.

To my mind, this practical function is the principal virtue of animated film and one which, paradoxically, makes it a true art. An artist, I believe, must always have a practical job to do. Only if his or her conscious mind is occupied with fashioning the work to that purpose can his or her instinctive feelings be freed to give, involuntarily, deeper qualities to the piece. The greater the blessing of inborn talent, the greater the art that will emerge. Even for those less blessed in this respect, a well-fashioned work of skill may still result. Employing, as it does, images, words, and music, animation is capable of anything. Go to it.

Drawn Animation Process

The diagram summarizes the traditional process of the production of an animated film. For the techniques of cutout animation, sand and paint over glass, etc., see the separate articles. The division of tasks illustrated has evolved from the need to divide the work between different people with different skills so that the time taken to make a film is commercially viable.

Steps 1, 2, and 3 lay the foundation of the film and provide, at 4 and 5, material from which the film can be planned. The animation director 6 takes the timing information on the dope sheet and the picture planning of the layout 7 for each scene and initiates the movement drawing. While the background 8 is finalized as a separate strand, the main burden of the film – the animated drawing of the action – works its way through a process of refinement 10 and 11 to 12. Once the movement drawings are satisfactory, they pass to cel workers who reproduce them in color on transparent acetate 13 and·14. The cels and the dope sheet are united with the background 15, and each scene is carefully checked before it passes to the camera. The camera operator reads from the dope sheet the background, the cels, and the camera move required for each frame as he shoots it 16. The film goes to the laboratory for developing and printing 17, and the printed scenes are edited against the sound 18 to produce the cutting copy (or "work print"). When all the component sound tracks have been similarly fitted to the picture, they are mixed together 19 into a single master sound track. The negative rolls now go with the picture cutting copy to be edited to match it, and from the cut negative, a properly graded final print is made 21. As a print with a combined sound track, this can be projected as film. For TV and video, it is usual to transfer from a separate mute print and the sound master.

The storyboard

Sound is recorde

The idea

Movement drawing on paper

Background painted on paper

Completed drawing entered on dope s

Cels and background come together

Exp
ser
pro

Cels and background combined on film

DOPE SHEET

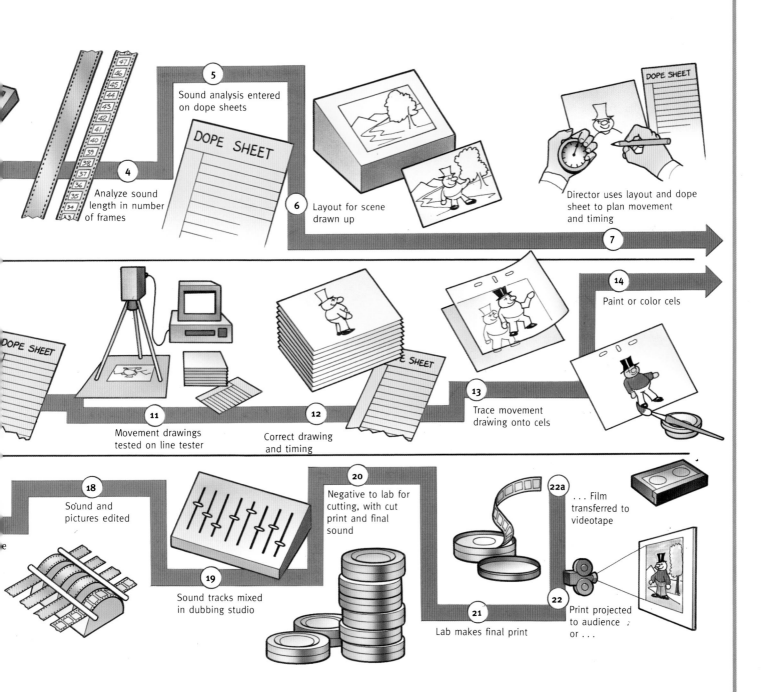

4 Analyze sound length in number of frames

5 Sound analysis entered on dope sheets

6 Layout for scene drawn up

Director uses layout and dope sheet to plan movement and timing

7

11 Movement drawings tested on line tester

12 Correct drawing and timing

13 Trace movement drawing onto cels

14 Paint or color cels

18 Sound and pictures edited

19 Sound tracks mixed in dubbing studio

20 Negative to lab for cutting, with cut print and final sound

21 Lab makes final print

22a ... Film transferred to videotape

22 Print projected to audience or ...

Computer Animation Process

Systems of production using computers vary in the extent to which traditional processes are taken over by computer work. For some, every stage past the initial planning is done by animators working on computers; for others, only the coloring of traditional drawn animation is done digitally. In all cases, however, the film – or video – rostrum is eliminated.

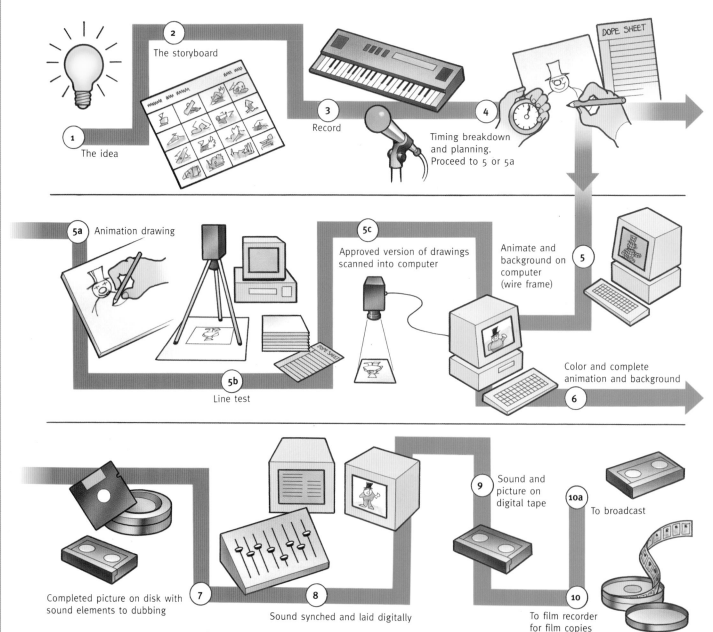

1 The idea

2 The storyboard

3 Record

4 Timing breakdown and planning. Proceed to 5 or 5a

5 Animate and background on computer (wire frame)

5a Animation drawing

5b Line test

5c Approved version of drawings scanned into computer

6 Color and complete animation and background

7 Completed picture on disk with sound elements to dubbing

8 Sound synched and laid digitally

9 Sound and picture on digital tape

10 To film recorder for film copies

10a To broadcast

Model Animation Process

The stages of production for model (or puppet) animation are similar to those for drawn work, but the specialized craft tasks are different.

Steps **1** to **4** in the initial planning and steps **9** to **14** of the post production stage are much the same as for drawn animation. However, film is more common as the medium for recording the movement, so there is less use of digital technology in that part of the process. The director takes the sound analysis of **4** and plans and times out the broad outlines of the action, scene by scene. Then, once the puppets and sets have been designed **5** and made **6**, they are brought together for shooting. The movement is created directly and spontaneously, frame by frame, in front of the camera **7**, either onto film or videotape **8**. The combining of the picture with sound follows a pattern similar to that of drawn animation.

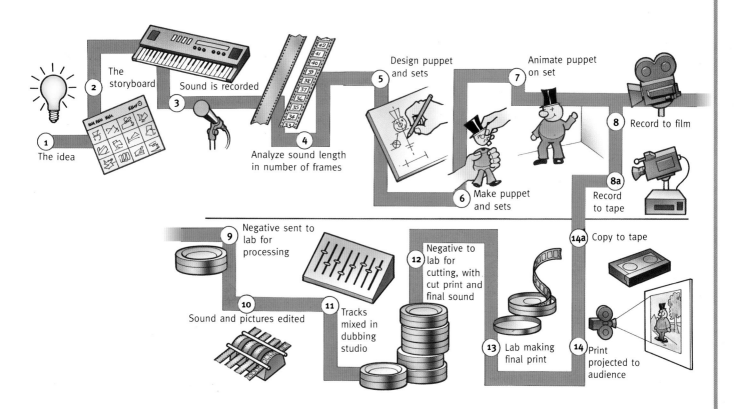

1 The idea
2 The storyboard
3 Sound is recorded
4 Analyze sound length in number of frames
5 Design puppet and sets
6 Make puppet and sets
7 Animate puppet on set
8 Record to film
8a Record to tape
9 Negative sent to lab for processing
10 Sound and pictures edited
11 Tracks mixed in dubbing studio
12 Negative to lab for cutting, with cut print and final sound
13 Lab making final print
14 Print projected to audience
14a Copy to tape

Conceptualization

It is impossible to define the concepts which guide the choice of subjects for animation. No sooner have you said "Animation can't do . . ." than an example will pop up to prove it can. Equally, if you say "Animation is best for showing . . .", you limit or devalue the other things it does. The chief characteristic of animation is the liberty it gives to choose any theme, presented through any image.

It is sometimes described as the "verse form" of film, as opposed to the "prose" of live-shot narrative and documentary, and this is true in so far as the images of live-action are gathered from the events of the world, while animation invents its world. An animated film can link images and follow a train of thought without regard to the logic of factual observation or real time. Another feature it shares with verse or poetry is that it often operates with symbols, analogies, and allegories. Donald Duck films are not about ducks; they are about people. Although Donald represents neither a duck nor a person, he serves to remind us of human characteristics in a way which could not be done either by a live actor or by a drawn character with a human appearance.

However, in recent years, animated film-makers have broadened their scope and are introducing new themes expressed in realistic images. It is now possible to envisage portraits of individuals made in animation, but the action would have to be imaginatively structured to give life and point to the portrait if it is to achieve more than can be done with live photography.

There have been films which carry the marks of autobiography while retaining the character of a true cartoon film. Youri Norshtein's *Tale of Tales*, Alison de Vere's *Black Dog*, and even Bob Godfrey's *Polygamous Polonius* are examples.

▲ The illustration, from a Poul Driessen storyboard, encapsulates animation's ability to subvert reality, while imposing a new logic of its own.

Structure

Animation is not only a depiction of actions and events; there must be an underlying logic – a narrative pattern. This pattern is essential.

Specific actions will arise from the theme you have chosen, but because you are working in time (unlike traditional painting and picture-making) one action or event must follow another and there must be some logic which connects them. This logic we call the story. Story does not necessarily mean only narrative. The term "story" would equally apply to the sequence of action in a film employing purely abstract shapes and colors.

If we want to construct a story which is more than just a chain of gags arising from the simple plot dynamic, we have to look at a more developed dramatic structure. It can be expressed like this: establish characters and situation; establish the agent of conflict; develop conflict; climax; resolution.

Let's take Red Riding Hood and the Wolf. We start off with Mother equipping Red Riding Hood with the goodies for Granny, and sending her off with the warning to watch out for the Wolf. Here we have established or mentioned all the main characters, and planted the worry about the Wolf. The story now turns to the Wolf. First twist in the plot. The Wolf demonstrates both his guile and his ferocity by tricking his way into Granny's cottage, and eating her. Thus the tension is heightened because we know Red Riding Hood is now heading for trouble. When she gets to the cottage, the inevitable climax is cunningly postponed by the dialogue exchange "Oh what a big . . . etc," and, "All the better to . . . ." This acts as a tease which further builds the tension, before the climax of Red Riding Hood getting eaten. There are various endings, but in most of them the woodcutter comes in as an unexpected saviour, bringing a resolution which leaves everyone happy, except the Wolf.

Of the elements in a narrative such as this, getting the situation established is the most important. From it stems your audience's ability to keep up with whatever follows.

SAMPLE STRUCTURES These plot analyses show how common the elements described are.

ADAM AND EVE

ESTABLISH CHARACTERS AND SITUATION — *God, Garden of Eden, Adam and Eve, apple.*

INTRODUCE AGENT OF CONFLICT — *Snake.*

DEVELOP CONFLICT — *Snake persuades Eve. Eve persuades Adam. Effects of apple – they feel the need for clothes. Clothes indicate to God their disobedience*

CLIMAX — *They are questioned.*

RESOLUTION — *Expulsion from Heaven*

OTHELLO

ESTABLISH CHARACTERS AND SITUATION — *Iago shown as resentful of Othello from the first.*

INTRODUCE AGENT OF CONFLICT — *Othello's marriage to Desdemona gives Iago his opening. Othello is insecure personally because he is inept with women, and publicly because he is black.*

DEVELOP CONFLICT — *Iago uses Cassio to make Othello jealous. He plants handkerchief as a clincher.*

CLIMAX — *Othello strangles Desdemona.*

RESOLUTION — *Othello kills himself when all is revealed. Iago, denied what would be a tragic end, (to be killed by a vengeful Othello), is left to mundane justice.*

Storyboards

The storyboard is initially the way in which you, as filmmaker, find out by drawing pictures how you are going to develop the action of the film.

But although this is its first function, it also provides a "blueprint" for other people involved in the making of the film. As you go along, you discover where there may be problems in making clear what is happening, or in finding satisfactory ways of presenting your theme. What will also emerge is the shape of the film—how much time proportionately will be devoted to each sequence.

COMPOSING THE FILM Although some development between storyboard and finished film is inevitable—indeed desirable—the storyboard is where you compose the final edited picture. Besides creating the framework for each scene, you are choosing the point in the action at which you are changing to a different view, or cutting to an altogether different location, and this constitutes the basic editing of the picture. Once you have sketched the storyboard and are clear in your own mind that everything is there in the best order, and framed more or less right, you could be ready to start production. That would assume, however, that you alone are concerned with the making of the film, and this is rarely the case. Even if there are no sponsors or commissioners providing funding, there are likely to be collaborators and assistants; frequently, there are both. These people will need a storyboard which makes it absolutely clear to them how the film is going to work.

Those working with you need complete details of each scene in the film—background, action, framing, and camera moves—and this leads on to another vital function of the storyboard. The timing of the film can be calculated by visualizing the action, as noted on the storyboard, with a stopwatch. This will give you both the length of each individual scene, as well as a total length for the film. All such timings should be entered on the storyboard. Where there is dialogue, the time taken to speak the words gives a partial guide, but it is the action which should determine the true timing. Timing the action is particularly important in the case of commercials, which have to be fitted to an exact

Further Information
☞
Scripts & treatment, p.20

FIRST STORYBOARD FOR DRAWN ANIMATION
The idea is to build a story showing differing reactions to an event. In this example, one character is anxious and nervous, the other impassive and inert. This is the animator's first attempt. On the next page, we show a revised version of this storyboard.

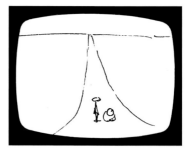

1 First frame establishes the characters and the location.

5 Fidget tries to interest his companion. The layout still helping to relate them to each other and the location.

6 Ball getting closer in a wide shot showing ball and characters.

10 Ball hits man.

11 Surprise! It bounces off him ...

NOTES FOR A STORYBOARD
In making the first notes for a storyboard, you do not need to stick rigidly to the proportions of the screen frame. As long as the flow and feel of action, and any sound, is clearly indicated, the picture format is irrelevant.

2 (On viewing the storyboard immediately, it was clear that a close-up to show one character fidgety, the other unmoving was needed.)

3 Something rolls over the horizon. Established in relation to them. This is the "agent of conflict."

4 Big close-up to demonstrate that this thing is a fearful threat.

7 Cut to direct profile of the characters to emphasize the direction Fidget wants the other to go as he pulls him.

8 Ball getting closer still. Framed like this, the tension is screwed up a notch from framing of 6.

9 Fidget runs for it. The layout gives room to see his action as well as behavior of the ball in 10 and 11.

12 ... but catches up Fidget as he is running along.

13 He is flattened.

14 His companion still calm.

Cleo Harrington's storyboard covers both the action of the live performer and the computer rendering to be added to tie in with the monologue. She needs to describe the planned action as a guide to the performer and also to make clear the effect of the computer animation to be superimposed.

REVISING A STORYBOARD
The storyboard on pages 16 and 17 is shown below in its next stage of development.

1–4 No change.

4a A close-up added to get a look at the approaching threat.

5 No change.

5a–5d As noted on the original, the interplay between the characters needs more time to develop and the suspense can then be built longer. In the original 6, 7 and 8, the ball and the characters were mainly shown together in the same frame. To do justice to the action of each, we now cut back and forth.

8 Similar to the original 8, but it now forms the end of 5d.

9–11 No change.

12a Extra frame for beginning of shot 12 to show Fidget running alone.

14 Left in, but this frame may be dropped.

time. At this stage it is useful to draw on detachable sticky labels or separate sheets, so that the frames of the storyboard can be changed, added to, taken away, or rearranged.

VARIATIONS Obviously the final storyboard for a model or puppet animation film will not bear such a close relation to the scenes as that for drawn animation. However, the framing and camera view for each scene should be defined in the storyboard.

PRESENTATION STORYBOARD There is a variation of the storyboard in which it is prepared for presentation purposes, and it is worked up with very much the finish of the final artwork of the film. Usually it is based on a condensed version of the action, since it would be too great a labor to work up every frame of a working storyboard. There is also a danger that, by taking projected illustrations for the finished film to a final stage, you kill the spirit before you have made the film.

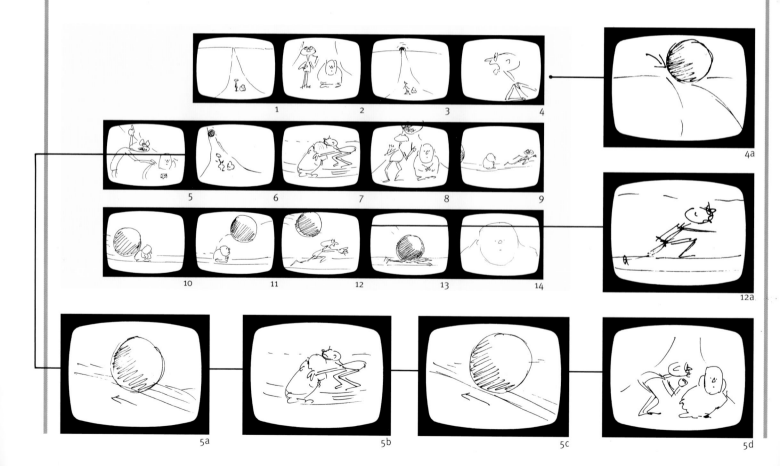

STORYBOARDS FOR MODEL ANIMATION

In comparison with drawn work, model animation is closer to live action, since once the puppet characters and their environment are built, they cannot be changed. Story development is by camera position and angle rather than by flexible re-drafting.

▶ This page of storyboard for a commercial by 3 Peach Animation with a road safety theme demonstrates how the action of the story is planned by visualizing the same character and environment from different angles and at different distances.

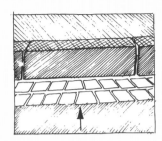

◀ ▶ This still of puppets shows how puppet characters develop from the storyboard. The concept of the principal character, however, was established before the storyboard was drawn; he shows less change than the models of the subsidiary ones.

Script and Treatment

A "script" usually means a dialogue script derived from the storyboard. A detailed written description of the action of an animated film rarely exists independent of the storyboard.

In making a series for television, episodes are sometimes prepared in the form of written scripts, but they are probably written within a context where the style and the characters are already established. Thus the likelihood of the script containing things which could not be animated successfully is reduced. The script should contain the words to be spoken by the voice artists, together with any stage directions necessary to describe the action and the mood. You should also, of course, be able to go through the storyboard with the actors and discuss the characters before recording.

The script should be clearly typed and the lines well spaced; actors like to mark up scripts with their own codes to make sure they find their cues and get the emphases and pauses right. Before recording, it is usually convenient to divide the dialogue into sections which can be edited together later. If the script is a long one —say more than 40 minutes—it may take more than a day to record, in which case recording the script in sections, out of order, can save the expense of having artists sitting idly by waiting for their section to come up.

TREATMENTS A "treatment" is a brief written description of a proposed film. In writing a treatment, you are trying to convey the impression the film will give, but before you have worked out the form or the detail of the action fully. Some sponsors or commissioning editors like to receive a written treatment of this kind, but it can present problems because you are describing the manner of a film before you know whether such a manner and such a film are feasible. Wherever possible, you should expect to present a practical storyboard rather than a hypothetical treatment.

Further Information
☞
Storyboards, p.16

DEVELOPING A TREATMENT

A treatment is a selling document. It should capture the spirit of the film you intend to make. Don't go into too much detail, but emphasize advantageous points; gloss over the low points. Treatment 1 is better than Treatment 2, which is more vague, seems not to have settled on a storyline, and is optimistic rather than realistic about means.

Harry the Train

A Treatment
Punk's answer to Thomas the Tank Engine

He may look like just an ordinary toy loco. But Harry's different from the others. Outlawed from the playroom, he hangs around under the Boy's bed with the other bad toys – headless dolls and battered and beaten up teddies. These low-lifers are out for revenge. They're taking no hostages. Massacre in the valley of the dolls...

The script will lend itself readily to the cut-out method, and this will allow for greater expenditure on good voice artists.

Harry the Train

A Treatment
Punk Rock's answer to Thomas the Tank Engine

With his slightly battered appearance, he may look like just another toy loco. But Harry's different from the other gleaming engines and tin cars. How he found his way into the playroom isn't clear. Probably he arrives on the dark side of midnight during a terrible electric storm or he may have been abandoned by previous occupants. He could be living in the attic when a young family move into the house. The little boy of the family finds the train and rejects it because it isn't as neat as his other playthings; he may subject it to a violent act, such as jumping up and down on it or painting it with his mother's nail varnish. Humiliated and angry, Harry embarks on a reign of terror, striking fear into the other playthings and causing havoc to the family.

We have not yet decided on the animation method but hope for full animation.

HARRY THE TRAIN

Character Sheet #124

"HARRY"

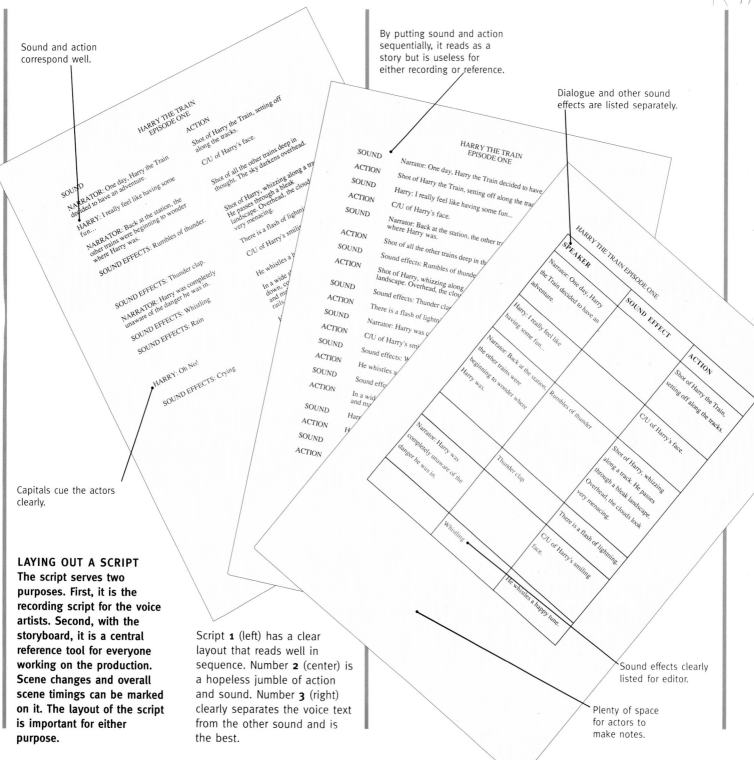

Sound and action
correspond well.

By putting sound and action
sequentially, it reads as a
story but is useless for
either recording or reference.

Dialogue and other sound
effects are listed separately.

Capitals cue the actors
clearly.

LAYING OUT A SCRIPT
**The script serves two
purposes. First, it is the
recording script for the voice
artists. Second, with the
storyboard, it is a central
reference tool for everyone
working on the production.
Scene changes and overall
scene timings can be marked
on it. The layout of the script
is important for either
purpose.**

Script **1** (left) has a clear
layout that reads well in
sequence. Number **2** (center) is
a hopeless jumble of action
and sound. Number **3** (right)
clearly separates the voice text
from the other sound and is
the best.

Sound effects clearly
listed for editor.

Plenty of space
for actors to
make notes.

Drawn animation

The colloquial term used by animators to distinguish drawn animation from puppet or 3-D is to call the first "flatties" and the second "lumpies." We are dealing here with the "flatties." All the techniques described in this chapter involve the creation on a flat plane of images which are successively changed or modified and the changes recorded to give the illusion of movement. In the case of normal drawn animation, cutout animation, painting on glass, and sand animation, all are produced by filming (or recording on video) the successive images with a vertically mounted stop-frame camera pointing down onto the horizontal picture plane. With direct drawing or scratching on film, a camera is not required, although a filming process is necessary to get a usable master image.

Computer animation is also a drawn technique, although the drawing tools are not the traditional paper, pencil, and paint. The successive images are again recorded to convey the illusion of movement, but this recording takes place within the computer. In order to be shown either on television or as projected film, the pictures must be transferred from disk onto either video tape or film.

Of the various drawing techniques described, the method of drawn animation with paper and cel is capable of the most precise planning. It is also the most suitable for being organized in a production process where the work is divided among several hands. Most of the animated films made between 1920 and 1990 have used this process to some degree, and it consequently has the most space devoted to it. Cutout, painting on glass, drawing in sand, and scratching on film are techniques more suited to the solo animator. Except for cutout, where some of the making of the flat puppets can be shared with assistants, the other techniques involve the direct filming of unrepeatable images.

▲ A picture to represent the classic age of Hollywood animation. "Tom and Jerry" from the MGM studio.

Tools and Equipment

Because you are drawing for the camera, your drawings must be in the same shape and proportion as the film frame, though not, of course, the same size.

The proportion (known as the Academy Ratio) is 1:1.376 which gives, as a typical average, a size of 12 x 8.72 inches. For television, the format varies slightly. The scanning area is slightly less than the full frame. Where titles are involved, an even greater allowance is needed.

REGISTRATION You will need a method of keeping your movement drawings in the same relationship to each other. The standard method is punched paper that fits over a set of pegs. The same pegs are also part of the camera table so that the drawings, when assembled for shooting, retain the identical positions. If you can't get hold of a peg-bar, crosses at the corners of the drawings can carry adequate registration, but it's a bit more difficult.

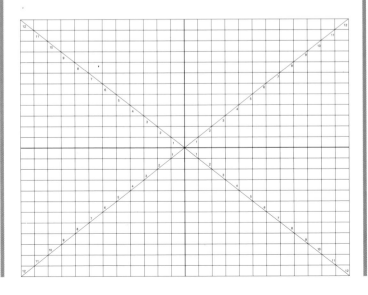

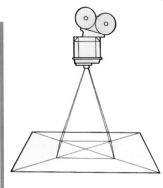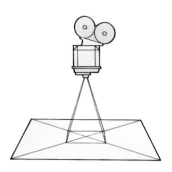

THE IMAGE FIELD
The field key is the essential tool for planning the size of field you wish the camera to cover, and the position of the field in relation to the camera center. The field that the camera photographs varies in size in relation to the height of the camera above the table.

▶ To make the camera appear to move across the drawing (picture) on the table, you must move either the drawing or the table on which it rests.

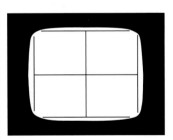

◀ This is a typical field key, or graticule. The fields can vary in size from 1 inch to 15 inches (and beyond) in breadth, but all are related to the camera center—i.e., where the diagonals from the corners cross at the center.

▲ ▲ The higher the camera is from the table, the greater the field, with a maximum of about 30 inches across. Fields as small as 2 inches can be achieved by bringing the camera down.

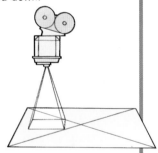

◀ The extent to which TV cut-off loses the edges of the academy field depends on the age of the TV set. Recent ones scan more of the field. In planning for television, particularly with titles, it is best to err on the side of pessimism.

WIDE-SCREEN FORMAT
Cinemascope and other wide-screen formats need different field keys for their slot shape.

DRAWING INSTRUMENTS The usual pencils, rulers, and erasers are used. Clutch pencils, which take 5mm leads of varying hardness, are frequently chosen since they don't need constant sharpening. Colored erasable pencils are useful for rough drawings, with the final line defined in black.

If you are finishing your animation as a single level on paper, you will find fiber-tip pens and colored markers useful, but be careful not to smudge the line with the color. You can avoid this by using water-based pen for the line, and spirit ones for the color, or vice-versa. Colored inks can be used, but they tend to wrinkle the paper. In addition, they make it difficult to get an even tone from frame to frame, which produces a distracting flicker or "boil" when they are filmed.

THE LIGHT BOX It is difficult to animate without working over a light, which allows you to see the positions of previous and succeeding drawings in order to judge those of further ones. It is also very useful when you are drawing the figure on several different levels of paper, since you can view all the levels at once when you need to.

PAPER The first stage of animation is usually done on paper. Almost any kind can be used, providing it is not too thin or too thick. As a rough guide, it should be thin enough for one or two drawings to show through when the box is lit, but not when the light is off.

Suitable paper can be bought from animation suppliers in quantities from packs of 50 sheets up to boxes of 1000. Photocopier paper is an acceptable substitute, but allows only a 9-inch camera field with a necessary adjustment to the camera center.

> **Further Information**
> ☞
> Backgrounds, p.46
> Cel, p.52

Backgrounds, p.46
Cel, p.52

THE WORKING ENVIRONMENT

For drawn animation, besides the light box and peg bar, an essential requirement is enough desk or shelf space close by, for the stacks of paper you have to manage.

There is the paper you are about to use, the drawings you have completed, and the dope sheets on which you keep a record of the animation. A big wastebasket is also needed for discarded roughs.

▲ The surface of a light box can be either glass or plastic, preferably frosted. Fluorescent tubes are cooler to work with. The angle of some light boxes to the working surface can be adjusted.

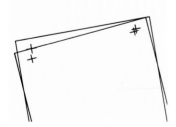

◀ Crosses as a substitute for peg registration. The crosses should be at least two of the corners of the sheets of either paper or cel, and preferably on all four.

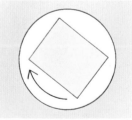

▲ On some light boxes, the central area is a disk which can be turned to position the drawing so it is reached easily. This is particularly useful for tracing and coloring.

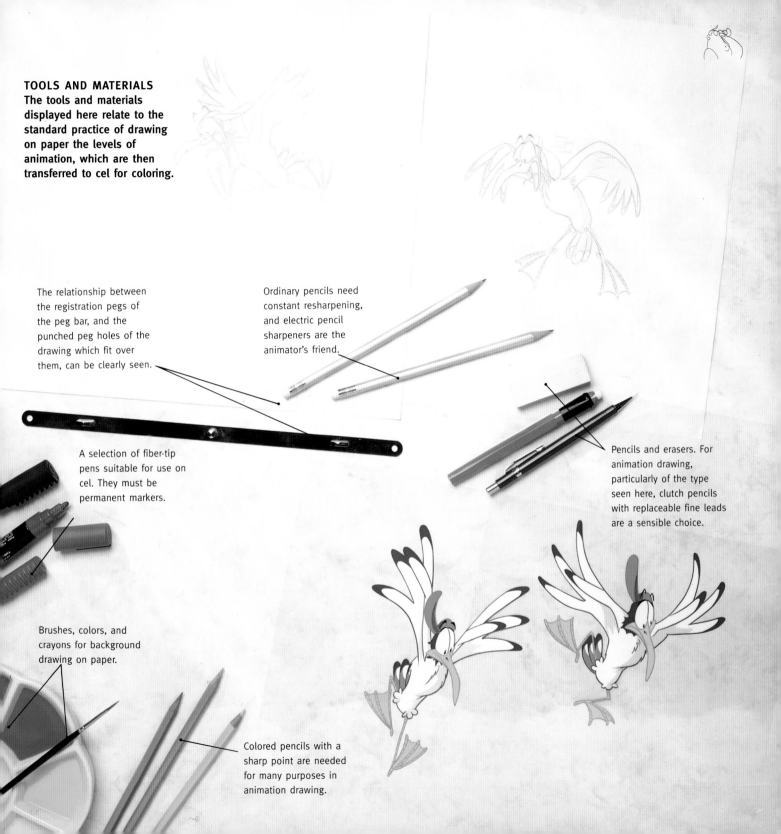

TOOLS AND MATERIALS
The tools and materials displayed here relate to the standard practice of drawing on paper the levels of animation, which are then transferred to cel for coloring.

The relationship between the registration pegs of the peg bar, and the punched peg holes of the drawing which fit over them, can be clearly seen.

Ordinary pencils need constant resharpening, and electric pencil sharpeners are the animator's friend.

A selection of fiber-tip pens suitable for use on cel. They must be permanent markers.

Pencils and erasers. For animation drawing, particularly of the type seen here, clutch pencils with replaceable fine leads are a sensible choice.

Brushes, colors, and crayons for background drawing on paper.

Colored pencils with a sharp point are needed for many purposes in animation drawing.

Rostrum Camerawork

The rostrum is a film (or video) camera anchored on a stand which varies in complexity, giving movement to the camera and the table on which the drawings are laid.

It is possible to film or record drawn animation with a very simple set-up—two tables securely joined together for the stand and a bright spot-bulb placed on each side providing the lighting.

However, this set-up will give you only one fixed field, unless the camera has a zoom lens, and even with that, tracking movements to make the image appear closer or farther away will be difficult to make smooth, frame by frame. The animation itself will have to be designed for a static peg position unless you are ingenious enough to construct rules which slide horizontally to give background panning movement.

A single-frame 16mm or even 8mm film camera is fairly easy to acquire. Video recording of frame-by-frame animation requires special recording equipment as well as a video camera. You must have either a video recorder adapted to work with a control unit or a computer to record the image onto disk. Disk-recorded animation has to be transferred to videotape to be played back on anything except the original computer display.

LIGHTING For the lighting, something in the region of 500 to 600 watts is desirable. Once a suitable exposure has been arrived at by testing for the chosen film stock and a satisfactory standard f-stop (usually 4–5.6), the lighting for filming or video-recording artwork remains standard for almost all shooting until a new film stock is brought into use. In drawn animation, the prime object is to avoid any fluctuations in photographic quality so that the scenes are all uniform. If under- or over-exposure is deliberately intended, it is normally achieved by altering the f-stop rather than the lighting. Using the variable voltage control to reduce or increase the lighting affects the color temperature.

Further Information
☞
Layout, p.42

WHAT THE ROSTRUM CAMERA DOES

With a simple homemade set-up of the kind shown below, you can film or record animation drawings in a limited way. It gives you a fixed relationship between the camera and the drawings and standard unvarying lighting. For full exploitation of the camera's potential, you need various refinements. To achieve apparent camera moves with artwork, you need to be able to move the camera vertically and the table horizontally and to have those movements precisely controllable frame by frame. Control of the shutter opening and the focus are also required. Such refinements are embodied in a rostrum camera like the one shown opposite.

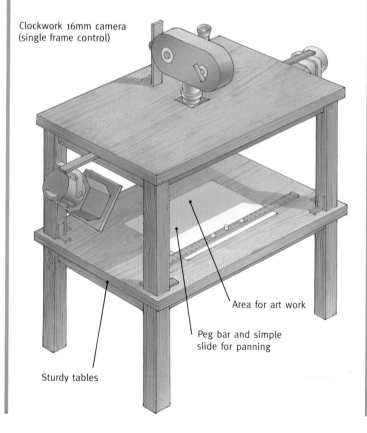

Clockwork 16mm camera (single frame control)

Area for art work

Peg bar and simple slide for panning

Sturdy tables

THE PROFESSIONAL ROSTRUM

Nowadays, most professional cameras and rostrums are adapted for computer control. All camera and table movements, even the panning rules on the table and the shutter controls can be programmed before shooting starts. This takes away from the operator the anxiety of remembering which handles to turn, frame by frame, and the moves themselves are more accurate.

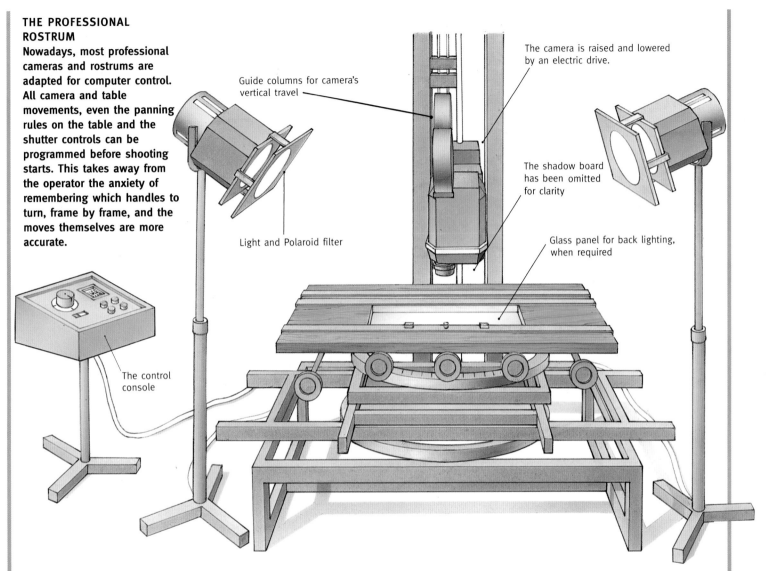

Guide columns for camera's vertical travel

The camera is raised and lowered by an electric drive.

The shadow board has been omitted for clarity

Light and Polaroid filter

Glass panel for back lighting, when required

The control console

The camera table is mounted on a stand about 3 feet high. It is capable of moving toward you or away from you (called north-south movement—north being at the far side of the table), and from left to right (west-east movement), or any combination of the two. The table can also be turned through any rotation up to

360°. The important and crucial requirement is that the camera, in its vertical travel, should always be true to the same center. All instructions relating to camera and table moves are based on that center. Most cameras are made so that they can be racked over to allow reflex viewing through the lens. Sometimes a

pantograph is attached to the table to indicate, on a separate field guide, where the camera center is in relation to the drawings on the table.

The table moves are controlled by handles on the stand. The switches and dials for the camera functions are usually on a separate console which can be moved to suit

the operator. The lights placed left and right of the table should have a separate control so that the voltage supplied to them can be varied. It prolongs the life of the light bulbs if the voltage to them is raised gradually when switching on.

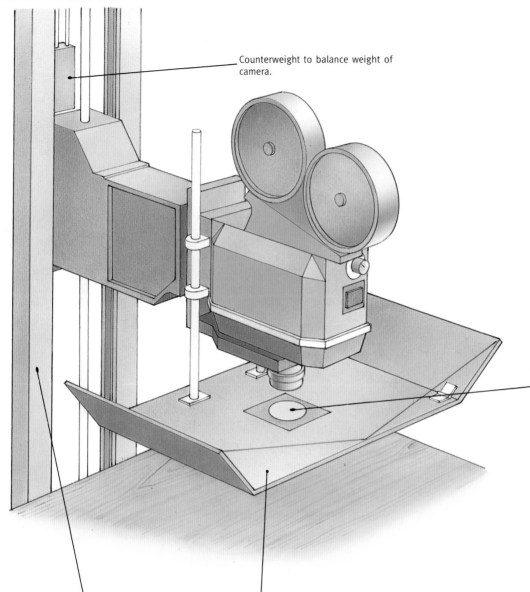

Counterweight to balance weight of camera.

CAMERA DETAILS
Mounted with the camera on the carriage is the stop-frame motor capable of turning the camera over for either a single-frame exposure or continuous shooting. The highest speed for such motors, though, is usually not more than 180 frames a minute.

Below the lens, in the opening in the shadow board, is a carrier for the polaroid filter which works in conjunction with similar filters on the lights to limit "scatter" rays coming from scratches on the cels or from dust. Also traveling with the camera carriage is the mechanism for maintaining focus.

Guide columns to ensure precise vertical travel.

Below the camera is mounted a board—the "shadow board," usually covered with black cloth. This stops the camera from being reflected in the cels or the glass of the platen. It is customary also to black the lens ring.

Since the aim of two-point lighting is for a flat response it is not easy to get any effects with reflective materials such as gold or silver foil, sequins or tinsel. If you want to do something with those you will need to abandon the standard lighting and the polaroid filters, then place a narrowly focused spot beam in such a way as to reflect the sparkle into the camera. Using the back-lit panel (see Table details, right) to get these effects with masks of various kinds placed on it, will almost always require testing beforehand to get the right f.stop and exposure.

TABLE DETAILS
The table is a piece of thick board about 2½ x 4 feet. Inset into this board are three engineered moveable rulers.

▼ The rulers have slots in them into which the pegs which give the registration of all cels and drawings are fitted. When the rulers are at center and the table is also centered, the field lying between the two nearer rulers is the standard 12-inch field.

By bringing the table forward (south) ⁹⁄₁₀ inch, the distance between the third ruler and the bottom one is now correct for a 15-inch field on camera center. These two centers are used for providing the standard field guides. Inset into the table between the

rulers for the 12-inch field is a glass panel which can be lit from below for backlit work. The three rulers are moved in fractions of an inch by worm drives under the board, controlled either by the handles on the board or by motors from a central computer.

Pressure glass in raised position. It is lowered to press down on the cels to eliminate shadow

Ring for revolving the table 360° if required.

Control wheels for moving the panning rules, one turn equals one-tenth of an inch

Control wheels for east/west and north/south movement of the table

TABLE MOVES
These are the basic directions of travel of which the table is capable. All these moves can be combined to get diagonal, curved or irregular paths of movement.

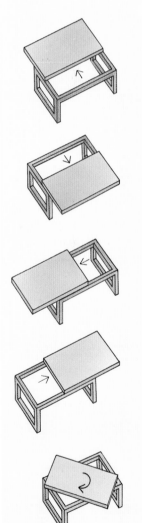

Characterization

The concept of the character you design relates very closely to what it is going to do and to the technique used for drawing it.

Your character is going to have to do various things: look and react; walk; use its hands; speak. These then are the essential elements. A perfectly satisfactory character could be animated using these aspects alone, but since characters relate to a story, and it is more comprehensible to an audience, these features are normally embodied in a complete figure. The proportions of the figure may vary, but it is important to remember that actions and expressions are easier to convey with some exaggeration. The standard head-to-body proportion for cartoon characters is often given as 2½:1 with an accompanying enlargement of hand and foot size. This is obviously only a guide—individual preference will determine what each artist does. These proportions do, however, suit the shape of the frame. If a long, thin character is shown at full height, the features and details will have to be drawn smaller.

DEVELOPING CHARACTER THROUGH MOVEMENT Virtually the only characteristics (as opposed to costume detail) that can be built into the design of a cartoon character are the capacity for movement or the lack of it. Other indications of temperament and disposition (wicked, good, clever, stupid) become evident from what the character *does*. What it does relates back to its capacity for movement.

GENDER IN CARTOON CHARACTERS It has to be admitted that in general animation has been largely "a boy's game," and female characters have been strictly in a minority. They tend to be gross stereotypes (sexy, shrew, grandmother) rather than individual characters. Minnie Mouse is Mickey in a dress. Only in recent years with the rise of women animated filmmakers has there been an improvement in the depth of character.

Further Information
☞
Storyboards, p.16
Continuity, p.56

DEVELOPING A CHARACTER Although you will probably begin to plan your film with some idea of what your characters are going to look

A RANGE OF STYLES
The variety in the character examples on this page reflect first, the intention behind each work, and second, the method of production employed.

▼ *Some Protection* by Marjut Rimminen. The story was based on a personal history, so the character design is partly a portrait. Again, an animator has worked solo or with few assistants, allowing a freedom of techniques.

▼ Maureen Selwood's *Flying Circus*. A solo artist able to maintain a loose line, in a film which used several techniques.

▲ *Animal Farm*, Halas and Batchelor. These characters are created for big unit work for a feature-length production. Their design is necessarily simplified, but they are successfully individual. There is a problem in keeping animal characters natural while giving them individuality.

▲ "Tom and Jerry," MGM. Here we have classic big/small opposition with a plot line to suit. The design is simplified so that it can be drawn uniformly by many animators through a series lasting several years.

▶ *The Simpsons* are also studio produced (Klasky-Czupo Productions) but with a totally different philosophy. Based on comic-book characters, they are designed to have markedly different outlines. Strong stories and dialogue make up for the limited animation. The fact that they are not lifelike makes them no less sympathetic in action.

▶ *The Frog King* also by Marjut Rimminen. In contrast to *Some Protection,* here she has designed for studio production, so the graphic treatment is simpler and employs conventional traced line and painted cel.

like, it is a good idea to keep the design sketchy while preparing your storyboard. Drawing the storyboard will take the characters through all the actions and surroundings they will have to cope with, and your view of the characters will develop.

After this, if the character design is for a series or large feature production where several artists are going to be drawing the same character, the animation director will draw up a definitive model sheet. This is for line drawing only. Color models are done separately. Besides specifying the proportions of the figure and indications of the way it should be handled in action, as well as its appearance from all angles, certain details can be dealt with—hand shape and behavior, eye and eyelid actions, mouth shapes— anything, in fact, which needs to be standardized.

DESIGN CONSIDERATIONS
The examples given here are not hard-and-fast rules, but they typify the considerations which influence the design and development of drawn characters.

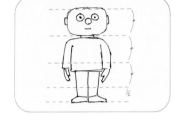

◀▲ The basic elements have to be incorporated in a complete figure. The rule of thumb proportions used for figure design are these.

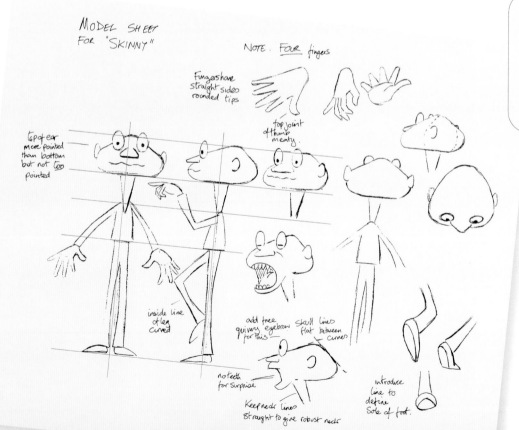

MODEL SHEET FOR "SKINNY"

NOTE. FOUR fingers

Fingershape straight sides rounded tips

top joint of thumb meaty.

top of ear more pointed than bottom but not too pointed

inside line of leg curved

add free quivery eyebrow for this

skull lines flat between curves

no teeth for surprise

Keep neck lines straight to give robust neck

introduce line to define sole of foot.

▲ Once a tall character is introduced, the details of a shorter character to go with it are reduced in size and prominence.

◀ This is an example of the sort of model sheet used to prescribe the proportions and details of a character for others to follow. It would also be amplified with some drawings of the whole figure.

DEVELOPING CHARACTERS

Let's suppose that you decide to do a story involving two characters—one lively and energetic, the other placid and slow moving. (You will have noticed from the character spread that where characters come in pairs, there is an attempt to show difference by clear contrast of shape and size.)

1

2

3

◄▲ These sketches show the gradual refinement and development of a character. 1 is the first attempt to present two contrasting characters. 2 shows the figures in action from the first rough storyboard and gives an impetus to shape development. 3 is the stage reached when the proposed action has all been gone through on the storyboard. Between 3 and the model sheets shown on this page and the opposite page, it is assumed that some trial animation has been done to achieve final definition of details.

MODEL SHEET   "DUMPY"

Note: Feet will be painted the same color as the rest of the body, Therefore line defining foot shape not always necessary

Note Three fingers

If arm moves Completely to side, do not separate from main shape Add hand to lump on outline.

This character rooted to the spot throughout. Movement therefore limited to changes in shape of mass.

Relative Sizes

Movement

Movement equals life; hence the term "to animate." But animation does not mean taking a still drawing and making it move. The intended action must come first, with the drawings planned to create that action.

The simplest form of action, and one people often begin with, is metamorphosis—the changing of one object or person into another. This goes back to the earliest experiments with cinema when such "magic tricks" were the main attraction. By experimenting with changes of this kind you can get a feel of the relationship between numbers of drawings and perceived time. The standard would be one drawing for every two frames of film, or 12 drawings per second. A slow change will take a lot of drawings, while rapid transformations can be done with fewer.

From alterations within shapes, you can progress to creating the illusion of an object, animal or person moving through a distance. The relationship between the number of drawings and time now has added to it the element of distance. To travel in screen 5 inches in 2 seconds (50 frames) means a movement of $\frac{1}{10}$ inch per frame (single framing this time) for an even movement. To slow down or speed up such a movement, you simply increase or decrease the distance travelled per frame.

Control of speed is the essence of animation. If all the moves are even and unchanging, the animation will be weak and lifeless. When someone kicks a ball, there would be no force to the kick if the foot were to swing evenly, so acceleration and slowing down are required. An understanding of actual movement is a necessary background to successful animation, as is some knowledge of anatomy. Drawing from life is a vital exercise, and a small library of reference books can add useful knowledge. The volumes of photographs by Eadweard Muybridge recording human and animal motion and published in the late 19th century, are particularly revealing. However, the idea that animation should aim "to imitate life" is a misconception. Live filming can take care of that. The power of animation lies in bending and accentuating time, speed and shape. Drawings should be spaced so as to express what you want them to do.

ANIMATING MOVEMENT
The principal aim in animating the movement of human or animal characters is to make believable—and expressive—the way in which the weight is carried and propelled by the limbs. Facial and gestural expressions are the final flourish of such movement.

▶ These are drawings by Monique Renault from her film *La Donna E Mobile*. Dance, particularly a dancing group like this, is a challenge to the ability to make movement graceful and credible. These are single-level crayon drawings on paper, with the background drawn with the figures.

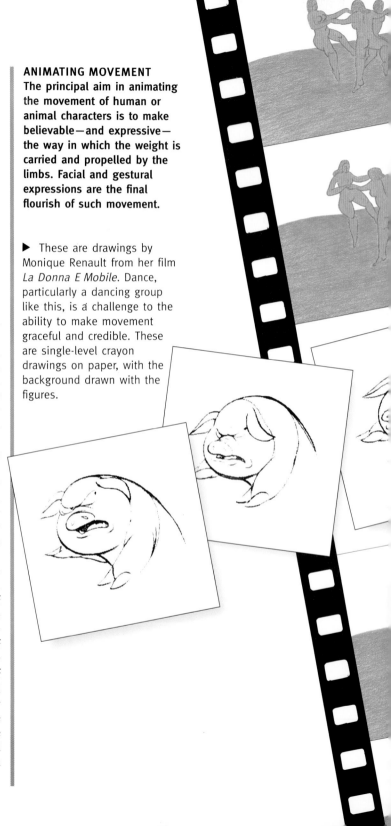

▲ A set of line drawings from the animation of the principal character from *Animal Farm* by Halas and Batchelor. The shift in weight of the mass of the pig's body and weight which climaxes with the facial expression is well demonstrated.

▶ *Lautrec*, Geoff Dunbar. Although the spirited drawings on which the film was based gave the animators a head start, it was the skill with which the movement was created that made the film alive. Drawing the action of the characters came first. Giving them the Lautrec "look" was the final gloss.

1

CONTROLLING MOVEMENT
Movement requires the control of both the change in shape or position of the drawings that make up the action, and the time that action takes.

▶ This metamorphosis is taken from a sequence in *When I Grow Up I Want to be a Tiger* by An Vronbaut. The entire sequence takes about 38 frames or 1½ seconds, in which a kitten becomes a large menacing tiger.

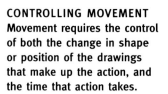

2

3

4

5

6

7

8

9

10

11

MOVING AN OBJECT
For moving an object, varying the rate of movement by the amount of change from frame to frame is the way in which expressive action is created.

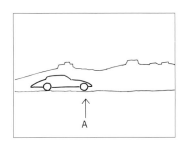 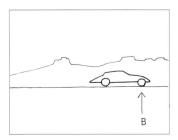

◀ Let us take the simple example of a car moving 5 inches across the screen from A to B.

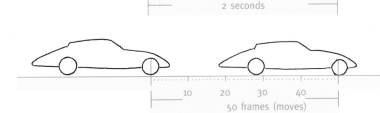

◀ If the car takes two seconds to move that distance evenly, it will have to be moved at ¹⁄₁₀ inch per frame for 50 frames.

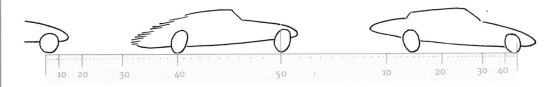

◀ If the car is to speed up or slow down in the same time and over the same distance, the move per frame will either increase or decrease like this.

SPEEDING UP AND SLOWING DOWN
Speeding up and slowing down are at the heart of imparting force to actions. Vigorous movements are given force by the spacing of drawings, as can be seen by comparing two kicking actions.

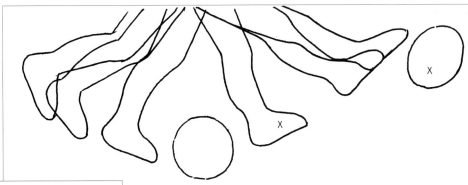

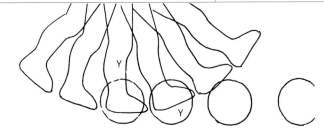

◀▲ Because the foot is at its fastest when striking the ball, there is no drawing of the impact position. The foot moves straight through, and the ball flies directly from its untouched static position (position X). By contrast (left) the foot swung evenly through can only manage to roll the ball along; Y shows the next frame after impact.

WALKING

This is a basic action, but one with many variations. In real life, a person's walk expresses character, and this can be reflected in the animation. The carriage of the body, arms, and head have to be considered with the feet and legs. In general, there is a high and a low position for a walk cycle. Think of the long-focus shots of crowds walking where the bobbing motion of heads can be seen most clearly.

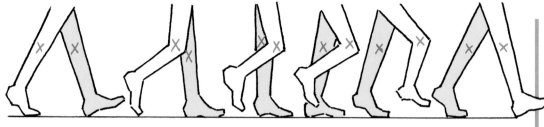

▲ A basic walk step with four in-betweens. This gives a ten-frame pace, or just quicker than two steps a second.

▶ As much as possible, you should avoid a middle position, since there is a danger, particularly with quick walks, of legs appearing to open and close like scissors.

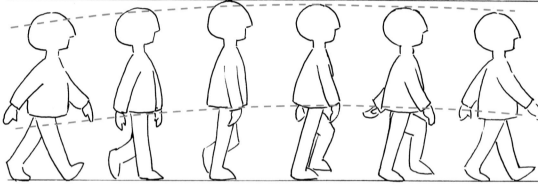

◀ From this example you can see that the high point comes while the grounded foot is the foundation of an upward push as the moving foot is brought through.

PERSPECTIVE MOVEMENT

We cannot within the scope of this book expect to provide a complete guide to drawn animation. There is, however, one further principle which is worth covering. Where a character or an object is traveling towards or away from the camera, it is not easy to recognize how disproportionate the apparent distance traveled is, as something approaches or recedes.

◀ If we suppose that the character is coming toward the camera at an even speed, over a notional 66 frames (or nearly 3 seconds), the halfway point, drawing No. 17, is shown here. By drawing diagonals, as illustrated, from the first and last positions, the mid-point is established by the intersection of the diagonals.

STRETCH AND SQUASH

This phrase refers to the distortion of the shape of an animated character or object to dramatize the movement being portrayed, for example the tendency to rise and fall through a walking movement. This emphasis should be sparingly used; continuous stretch and squash can be an irritating stylistic tic and give a soft and boneless feel to drawn animation.

The figure, which in 5 is compressed and bulging at the start of the hauling move, is exaggeratedly stretched at the end of it to dramatize the resistance of what is being pulled.

WALKING ON THE SPOT

Often, a character must remain in the same place in the frame while appearing to move in relation to the background scene. The walk is animated so that the foot which is in contact with the ground slips back by the same amount that the background moves, and in the same direction.

The illustration shows a pace measuring about 1 inch from heel to heel, and there are five drawings in each pace. For each drawing in the cycle, therefore, the foot slips back two-tenths of an inch. Since it is usual for the background to move in every frame (although the animation drawings are each used for two frames), we can assume that the background for this walk moves from right to left at one tenth of an inch per frame.

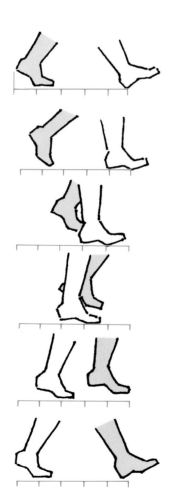

ANIMATING BIRD FLIGHT

There being no ground surface to support a bird, the body sinks at 1 where the wings are completely up compared with 5 where the force of the downward flap has raised it. This is an even cycle with the same number of drawings as the wings come down as when they go up. For a more forceful action you would make the downward flap shorter than the up.

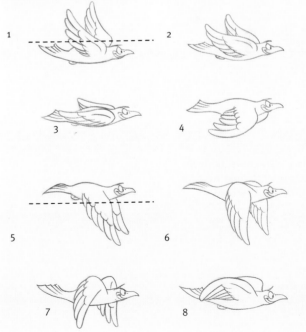

SPACING AND TIMING
This series of drawings of a throwing action shows how the spacing of drawings through a movement and the number of frames assigned to each drawing govern the movement.

1

2

3

4

10

11

12

13

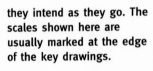

14

MOVEMENT KEY
It is usual to express the spacing of the drawings which governs the speed by a "movement key." These are standard practice for key animators to guide their assistants in the spacing of in-betweens, but they are also used by animators working on their own to make a note of the speeds they intend as they go. The scales shown here are usually marked at the edge of the key drawings.

1
2
3

4

4
5
6
7
8
9
10

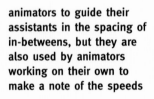

10
11
12
13

14

14

15
16
17

Drawing 4 is regarded as a half-key. It comes at the middle point of the crouching action. 3 is half-way between 1 and 4. 2 is half-way between 1 and 3.

As the move slows, 6 is half-way to 10. 5 is half-way to 6. 7 and 8 are thirds of the distance between 6 and 10. 9 is half-way between 8 and 10.

The actual distance travelled between 10 and 14 is the greatest, as they are the extremes of the throwing action. 13 is the half-way. 11 and 12 are halves again.

The carry through of the action means that 15 is a full half-way through to 15 and 16 comes in to slow up to the final rest at 17.

5　　　　　6　　　　　7　　　　　8　　　　　9

15　　　　　16　　　　　17

ANALYZING TIMING

In detail, the timing for the sequence, above, is arranged thus:

1–4	A slow to fast move into the beginning of the crouch
4–10	Slow down as the figure compresses itself, indicating the increasing effort
10	Maintain this drawing as the pause before the throw
11–14	The rapid acceleration to project the ball
15–17	The drooping of the arm and the trail of the rear leg to follow through after the throw.

If these drawings were expressed in terms of frames, the doping for camera would go like this:

drawings 1 – 9	2 frames each	18*
10	8 frames	8
11	2 frames	2
12	1 frame	1
13	1 frame	1
14 – 17	2 frames each	8*
		38 frames

*Ignoring the initial pause on the start position and the held finish position.

THE DOPE SHEET

While the movement keys prescribe the spatial relationship of the drawings to each other, the dope sheet is where the drawings are given their timing by assigning a specific number of frames to each drawing. Each line on the sheet represents a frame of film. The doping for the action above is shown (right).

▶ When an animator is working with an assistant, he or she begins by marking the numbered keys on the sheet to define the timing. The assistant follows this and fills in the in-between drawings. The dope sheet is the essential document in animation production.

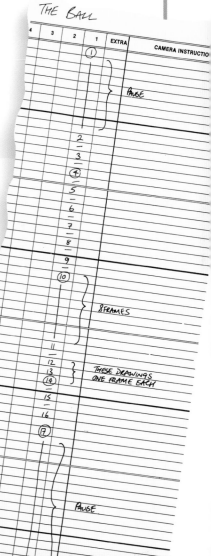

Layout

The layout takes each scene presented in the storyboard and turns it into an actual-size plan which will be the basis of both the background and the animation.

The layout artist makes a detailed line drawing of the background scene on pegged paper fixing the camera center and field size for the eventual shooting. Separately, on pegged paper over the top of the background drawing, he roughs in the characters at the right sizes and positions for the action of the scene.

In normal studio production, the drawing and painting of the final background is not done by the animators, but by a different set of people. Each group works separately, and the final cels of the animation and the completed background come together only at the checking stage before shooting. A great deal of the animation will relate directly to the background. For example, a character may pass out of sight through a doorway in the background. Animator and background artist must be provided at layout stage with the same match-line of the doorway edge. Even if you are working alone and intend to do both background and animation yourself, a layout for each scene, with the camera field defined and proper matchlines set, is essential.

Further Information
☞
Storyboards, p.16
Backgrounds, p.46
Cel, see p.52

1

2

7

8

FROM STORYBOARD TO LAYOUT
This commercial made by Grand Slamm for Cadbury's Caramel demonstrates how layouts are derived from storyboard frames.

▲ These frames cover the entire 30 seconds of action. The storyboard is highly finished, with a lot of final detail already defined.

▶ This is the background for scene 11, where the line of the cliff edge is the crucial element. We have shown the background with the field key over it, to illustrate how the layout fixes the scene for camera center and field size. (See p.44 for the doping of this scene.)

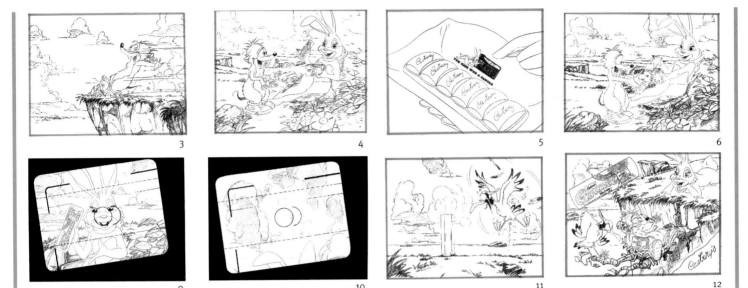

► The layout for the final scene (scene 12) involves all three characters. Besides making the match line where the lemming fits into the seagull's nest, the layout artist has modified the character's size and position from the storyboard frame to make sure all the action will work properly within the frame. (The final set-up as shot can be seen under CEL on page 52 where the buildup of the cel levels is demonstrated.)

CLOUD	BIRD	LEMMING		
✕	✕	1A	(BG 11)	
		2		
		3		
		4		
		5		
		6		
7C		7		
8		8		
9	1B	BLANK		
10	2			
11	3			
	4			
12	5			
13	6			
14	7			
15	8			
16	9			
17	10			

MATCHLINES
The importance of the match line can be seen from the illustrations on this page for scene 11.

◀ ▶ The action of the lemming disappearing over the cliff edge leaving a puff of dust is covered in pictures 1–4. We have used the animation drawings 6A, 7A, 8A of the lemming and 9C of the cloud. These represent the central part of the action, as can be seen from the dope sheet, shown left. Both background and animation drawing are on the same bottom pegs. If both use the same match line accurately, the final cels and background, although developed separately, will come together properly.

1

2

3

4

LAYOUT FOR A PANNING BACKGROUND

This is the layout for the action of scene 1 shown on the storyboard on p.42.

▼ The storyboard frame shows the action as it is at the end of the scene. This scene has the lemming running to the cliff edge throughout the action. Because the pace of the lemming's run is 0.7 inch per frame and the number of frames in the scenes is 56, the panning distance A to B can be calculated as 40 inches. This covers the distance of five field centers marked on the layout centers A, B, C, D, E, F. The lemming's relationship to the background at the start and end of the scene is indicated by rough keys.

SETTING UP A TRAVELING BACKGROUND

When a character is to appear to travel while remaining in the same place in the screen, the background must be extended to provide the apparent distance traveled.

▶ The diagram shows how a panning or traveling background is set up for the camera. The background is fitted to the pegs of the nearer panning bar on which it will be moved along the required distance for each frame. The cels of the running character are pegged to static pegs.

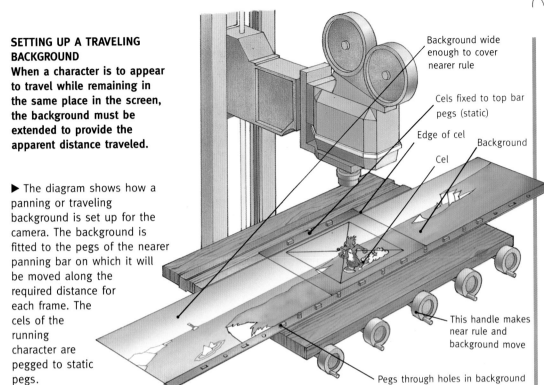

Background wide enough to cover nearer rule

Cels fixed to top bar pegs (static)

Edge of cel

Cel

Background

This handle makes near rule and background move

Pegs through holes in background

Backgrounds

The background is the element which is most like a conventional "picture." Stylistically, the main consideration is to achieve a marriage of technique between background and character.

With early work such as that of Winsor McCay or Messmer's *Felix the Cat*, this problem was minor, as both figure and background were simplified black and white drawing, but with Disney and the introduction of color, a potential conflict became evident—between the flat coloring on cel of the figure and the rich textures of the moody backgrounds.

An aspect of the rethinking of cartoon films represented by the work of UPA was in their treatment of backgrounds. Just as movement was minimalized and made more formal, so were the backgrounds. Naturalism and spatial definition were abandoned in favor of more abstract symbols and textures to convey a scene. In some cases in the '50s and '60s, all background details were abandoned, and the space in which the action occurs was simply a limbo defined solely by the characters' actions. This approach can strengthen the action, as it is not impeded by fussy detail; all arts benefit from giving the audience some scope for imagination.

Since the end of the '60s (roughly from the time of *The Yellow Submarine*), the use of illustrated books as a basis for animated films has brought together the treatment of figure animation and backgrounds. It has been helped by technical developments, such as frosted cel which accepts rendered textures, and by an increasing level of skill and adaptability among studio cel workers.

CREATING A BACKGROUND The section on layout on page 42 describes how the scenes are prepared from the storyboard for the separate work of animation and background. That preparation is to make sure that when the cels and the background come together for the camera there will be no problems.

STYLING The degree of background detail prescribed in the layout can vary a lot. Apart

Further Information
☞
Tools and materials, p.22
Cel, p.52
Layout, p.42

VARIETY OF APPROACH
The examples on this page show a range of techniques, from the lushly pictorial to the necessarily abstract. In all cases the designer has tried to achieve a suitable marriage between foreground action and the background. This problem is more easily solved by those working alone, or virtually alone—for example in *The Frog*—because the same hand and brain execute both elements. In *Heroic Times,* the background comes from large studio productions with the background artists working independently of the animator, and the control of background design results in blander formulas.

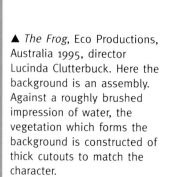

▲ *The Frog*, Eco Productions, Australia 1995, director Lucinda Clutterbuck. Here the background is an assembly. Against a roughly brushed impression of water, the vegetation which forms the background is constructed of thick cutouts to match the character.

◀ In this set-up from *Heroic Times* by Hungarian, Jozsef Gemes at Pannonia Film, the aim is to provide realism both in figure and background. With the action cel removed, the landscape can be seen to be drawn in soft focus to prevent it conflicting with the foreground.

▼ This is a more abstract design from *Heroic Times*. Here the action cels are so strong and so freely treated that the only background needed is a blur of color which blends with the cel work.

◀ *The Secret of Nimh* by Don Bluth. A background from a sophisticated production process. Back lighting and overlay levels help the intensity of the contrast between light and shade creating the spooky atmosphere. Stylistically, it is at odds with the cel characters.

PAINTING A BACKGROUND IN WATERCOLOR

The use of paper backgrounds for cel animation makes watercolor a natural choice of medium for coloring them. Background artists became skilled at painting naturalistic scenes in a manner which complements the flat colors of the painted action cels. Tonally, they are controlled to remain properly "in the background."

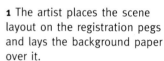

1 The artist places the scene layout on the registration pegs and lays the background paper over it.

from the essentials, the background artist may be allowed a relatively free hand, though the design must conform to an overall concept which has been laid down from the beginning of production. Early on, director and designer, if they are not the same person, will have agreed a set of concept designs for all the principal scenes and locations, together with rules about treatment of details and the use of textures or shading. Also, where there is any degree of realism, the backgrounds must follow from one to another with a degree of continuity.

To produce an ordinary conventional painted background in either gouache or watercolor, the procedure is this. The artist takes the pegged layout and if necessary completes the details of the drawing, taking care to observe the match lines. This drawing is then transferred to a piece of punched background paper of the right size, and the layout is transferred precisely to it, either with carbon paper or by tracing from the layout over a light box. With watercolor it may be necessary to stretch the paper on a drawing board to prevent it from buckling. If the paper is stretched, the peg registration and the match lines must be rechecked after the background is finished to make sure that they still coincide.

PERSPECTIVE ILLUSION There is a refinement of panning background work where an illusion of perspective depth is created by making the background element in two or even three levels which move at different speeds. Those elements appearing nearest the camera will move at the greatest speed, those in the middle distance will move slower, probably at a speed which relates to any figure

2 The lines of the background are traced onto the paper from the layout, including the important match line of the cliff edge.

3 Using a selection of brushes, the artist begins a foundation wash for the grass surfaces.

4 The different green tones which mark out separate areas of grass are worked on.

7 Grass foreground detail is added . . .

8 . . . and the clouds are given volume against a delicately shaded sky.

9 This is the completed background with full light and shade in the sky and the landscape.

5 The sea is laid down initially as a flat wash.

6 Light and shade for the rocks and cliff.

Full color gouache.

Soft crayon.

Marker.

animation, while the far distance will move very slowly or not at all. Such arrangements mean all three bars on the rostrum table must be used, and the pegs have to be removed from one of them.

If you do contemplate a scene with action of this kind, it is a good idea to plan for cutaways during the action so that the panning scenes are reasonably short. Otherwise, the length of the cels and other art work can get out of hand.

MULTIPLANE SET-UP Perspective illusion of this kind is normally limited to two levels in drawn animation, although three, or even four, can be handled if there is no figure animation to occupy a set of pegs. Further illustration of depth can be created by using a multiplane set-up on the rostrum. The illusion is reinforced here because some of the planes are necessarily out of focus, whereas with the drawings all on the same plane, there is only a single focal plane.

REFERENCE MATERIAL All background artists are given, or make for themselves, ground plans or even three-dimensional models of the areas for which they are drawing backgrounds. In this way, particularly with long narrative films, they can make sure there are no discrepancies in the size or placing of objects in a room, or features in a landscape.

Like theater designers, the background artist is required to provide settings with buildings or plants or other features which should have a convincing accuracy of appearance. A library of reference books on natural history, architecture, and social history is useful. A scrap collection drawn from photographs, illustrations from magazines, and postcards can be an added asset.

DIFFERENT TREATMENTS
These examples, 1 in full-color gouache; 2 in soft crayon, and 3 in line only, show how the same scene can be differently rendered, perhaps to suit different ways of coloring the cel, but all provide the information for the action.

ILLUSION OF DEPTH

The illustrations on this page all relate to creating the illusion of depth of perspective, either by moving different levels of the background at differing speeds, or by actually placing the elements of the picture at different distances from the camera.

▼ Sheets of glass are mounted at varying heights above the rostrum table and the camera focuses on only one of them, perhaps only on the table level itself. Art work on the other levels will be proportionately out of focus. Since the camera field reduces in size as the drawings are situated closer to the camera, they should be planned accordingly. Limited camera and table movement are possible, but with difficulty.

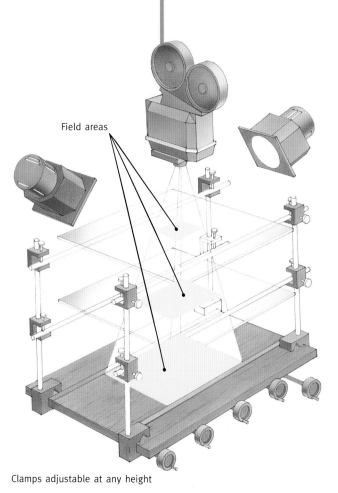

Field areas

Clamps adjustable at any height

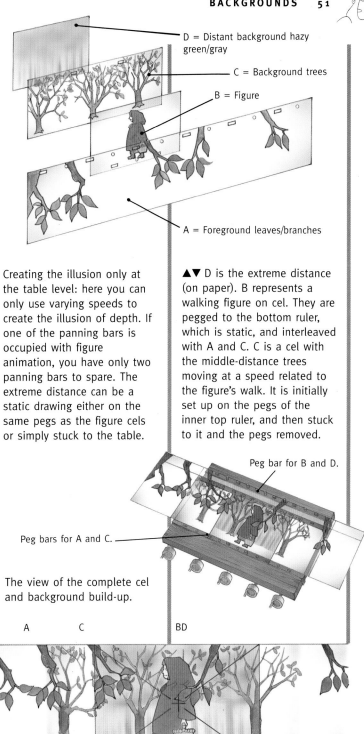

D = Distant background hazy green/gray

C = Background trees

B = Figure

A = Foreground leaves/branches

Creating the illusion only at the table level: here you can only use varying speeds to create the illusion of depth. If one of the panning bars is occupied with figure animation, you have only two panning bars to spare. The extreme distance can be a static drawing either on the same pegs as the figure cels or simply stuck to the table.

▲▼ D is the extreme distance (on paper). B represents a walking figure on cel. They are pegged to the bottom ruler, which is static, and interleaved with A and C. C is a cel with the middle-distance trees moving at a speed related to the figure's walk. It is initially set up on the pegs of the inner top ruler, and then stuck to it and the pegs removed.

Peg bar for B and D.

Peg bars for A and C.

The view of the complete cel and background build-up.

A   C   BD

Cel

It is a paradox that the definitive form of the animation—the cels—are normally executed by the lowest-ranked artists in the studio.

Occasionally animator/directors work on the final cels themselves, but this stage usually happens only on short films of personal interest to the filmmaker. In normal commercial production, the cels, if they are still hand-traced and colored, are several steps removed from the originating artist.

Cel, a thin, transparent acetate, is an unresponsive substance on which to draw, but it is essential to drawn animation as a means of avoiding unnecessary work. Without cels, the animator is confined to a single level of paper, drawing and redrawing the entire scene for every other frame—12 for every second. In standard cel work,

THE USE OF CELS

Early in the history of cartoon films, various attempts were made to avoid the tedious labor of redrawing the entire scene for every movement drawing. With the advent of transparent celluloid (hence "cel"), the problem was solved. A single background could be used with all the movement drawings of a scene.

◄ The cel buildup for this scene is demonstrated schematically here. The background is at the bottom, and the various levels are in order above it.

1 This is the background alone, without cels.

2 The first level is a shadow. By reducing this shadow to only 40% exposure, the dense blackness is reduced.

3 The bodies of the rabbit and the lemming do not move, so they form the first character level. Note that the lemming's body matches the edge of the nest.

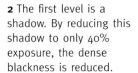

ACTION	DIAL	EXTRA	8	7	6	5	4	3	2	1	EXTRA
									6	13	
									7	14	
									8	15	
									9	16	
									10	17	
					①E	①D	①C	①B	①A	SC 12	15" FIELD ¢
take	A Y					2	2	2			
	K					3	3	3			
it	ℓℓ					4	4	4			
	D					5	5	5			
easy	ℓℓ					6	6	6			
						7	7	7			
						8	8	8	1A		
	Z					9	9	9	T		
	ℓℓ					10	10	10			
						11	11	11			
	N					12	12	12			
							13	13			

DOPING CEL LEVELS

Without a dope sheet, the cels, no matter how carefully numbered, would be a meaningless heap. On the dope sheet they are organized frame by frame in the correct relationship with each other to create the action as planned.

▲ The dope sheet reads bottom to top from right to left, each line representing a frame. The static shadow and the bodies are at the bottom (ignoring the pack). Then the levels of heads and the bird, which change frame by frame, are doped in order.

the cel is laid on the registration pegs over the drawing, and the lines are traced on the front. It is then turned over for coloring, and flat areas of color, usually made with acrylic or vinyl paint, are filled in on the traced areas in accordance with a color model already established for the production. Unless the tracing is very precisely done, the animation drawings will be debased at this final stage. In some studios, photocopying onto the cel means the animator's line can be transferred directly, but there is still troublesome labor involved in preparing the drawing before copying, and in the cleaning and registration of the photocopied cel.

MATERIALS AND METHODS The glazed surface of normal cel rejects some drawing materials, particularly if they are water-based. Lines can be traced with either diluted acrylic paint applied with a fine brush, or a variety of permanent felt-tip pens and markers. Drawing pens like mapping pens give a varied line, while tubular-nibbed drafting pens give a line of even thickness. Tracing with a brush is usual for making a line the same color as the painted areas. Nearly all the lines made by pens or felt-tips are black.

Transparent drawing ink, sometimes used to give a texture to a colored area, must be permanent; glass ink is an example, but it takes a long time to dry. Ordinary crayons or colored pencils will not make a mark on cel, but wax or oil crayons will; and quite pleasing effects can be gained by drawing either on the front or back with wax pencils (china markers). The choice of colors is

4 The lemming's head and hands are the next level.

5 The rabbit, which speaks in this scene, is the next level.

6 Finally the seagull completes the buildup of five levels (excluding the shadow).

WORKING ON CEL

The first stage in transferring the drawing to cel is to define the areas to be painted. The tracer places the cel over the drawing and traces accurately the line in whatever medium is specified. Generally, this is a matter of accurately reproducing the line drawing without degrading it.

Waterproof felt markers give a firm black line on cel. They are quick and easy to use, but for fine detail they are crude.

Mapping pen, tracing here with diluted paint (although ink could be used) to give a fine line.

Brush tracing can give the finest line of all, but it needs a steady hand.

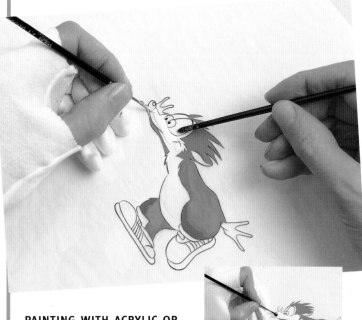

PAINTING WITH ACRYLIC OR VINYL PAINTS

When the finished tracings have been checked, they are passed to the painters (or colorists). The paint is applied to the back of the cel so that the front surface will show a flat, unbroken color. To keep brushmarks from showing, the paint is applied as a thin liquid, but thick enough to be opaque.

Applying the paint is called "puddling." Paint in the consistency of thin cream is conveyed on the brush to the area to be colored. The inset shows the brush being used to push the paint to the edges of the area to be colored.

small, but this limitation can be overcome by blending them on the cel. The resulting drawing is not opaque, so it may have to be backed with paint.

Cel work is a skilled craft, and the excellence of many films has depended on the quality of the tracers and colorists who have worked on them. The technique of putting the paint on the cel for instance, requires considerable practice; it depends on diluting the paint to the right consistency and "puddling" rather than brushing it on. The brush is used to guide the liquid paint into the edges of the area to be colored. If the paint is too thick and sticky, the brushmarks will be seen and the paint surface will be uneven, giving an undesirable buildup when levels of cel are put together.

FROSTED CEL There are cels with a slightly frosted surface which accept all drawing materials, including watercolor and colored pencils. These cels are expensive and, because of the frosting, will tend to degrade the background if more than two levels are used. If more levels are unavoidable, the cels can be sprayed with lacquer when the drawing is complete, to render the rest of the cel clear again. Alternatively, ordinary cel can be treated with a solution which gives a similar surface to frosted cel. This is sprayed onto the area of the design to be rendered, and can be shaded and colored as desired while the rest of the cel remains clear.

With recent advances in technology, the demand for these skills is likely to decrease. It is becoming common in larger studios to take hand work no further than the finished pencil stage of animation. Cel work and rostrum shooting are replaced by digital coloring of the animation drawings and recording them onto disk. The results do lack something in appeal, rather like synthesized music lacks the verve of music from traditional instruments.

WAX CRAYONS

China markers and wax crayons will make a mark on cel, where ordinary crayons do not. They are not capable of fine lines and, if used with line at all, the line should be strong and bold. They can, however, also be used on the back of a cel to shade areas, in a painterly fashion, without line. This technique works best with only one level of cel and results in a tonal fluctuation from cel to cel.

Here, the wax crayon is being used to add shading, or rendering, to the front of an already traced and painted cel. Wax crayon is not opaque, so it needs paint backing.

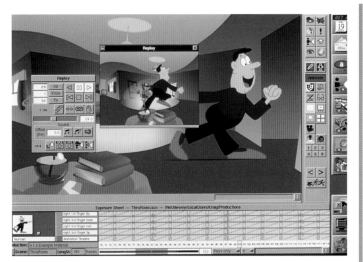

DIGITAL TECHNOLOGY

Applying digital technology to the coloring of animation was the next step after using it to control the rostrum camera. For productions where there is a large volume of drawings of the same character, as in series work, digital coloring has largely replaced the armies of cel workers.

▲▼ Animo, the system developed by Cambridge Animation Systems, is one of the most widely used techniques for coloring. Animation drawings on paper are scanned onto disk, and whole sets of an animated character can be colored at one time. The menus show a wide selection of shades and textures are available.

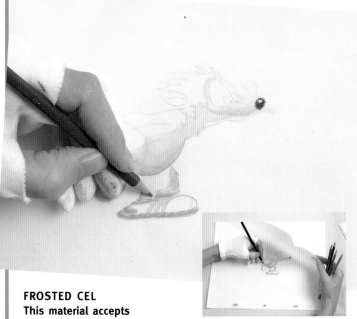

FROSTED CEL

This material accepts watercolor and ordinary pencils. It looks frosted in the hand, and when laid down, it is marginally more dense than normal cel. Ordinary cels can be sprayed or painted with a solution only on the area to be rendered. The solution gives the same effect as frosting.

The rendering on frosted cel can be much more delicate than with wax crayons. The slightly opaque nature of frosted cel is evident in the inset.

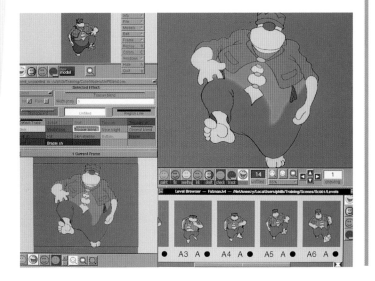

Continuity

In live-shot films, careful watch has to be kept that characters, costumes, and position in relation to the locale do not change from one scene to the next.

This is a danger where two adjoining scenes may be shot many days apart—and even in different places. Gross problems of this kind do not bedevil animation; a character inadvertently changing one or more of its colors due to wrong cel-painting is normally taken care of by the checking process.

CHECKING FOR CONTINUITY ERRORS The two main sources of error are line quality and coloring. The color model made at the beginning of production specifies these, and all cel work is expected to conform to it. Enough paint for all the projected cel work should be mixed, stored, and labeled ready for use. If any of the colors run out before the film is finished, extreme care must be taken in matching the new color to the old.

Although the final checking of each entire scene (all the cel levels and the background with the dope sheet) before it is shot is the most crucial, work is checked at each stage in the production. The key animator checks the assistants' work and the in-betweens. The drawings are checked again before tracing for errors and omissions, and the traced cels are usually checked before painting.

KEEPING CHARACTER Much the most serious and difficult continuity problem for animation is called "keeping character." Even if there is a character model sheet with detailed notes on line treatment, considerable variations may occur when different animators and assistant animators are drawing the same character. Animation directors have to be aware of this problem and pick up the most glaring examples at key-drawing or line-test stage.

It is not only in the manner of drawing that character variations can occur, but also in the movement. For instance, if a character has a particular walk —perhaps spring-heeled or leaden-footed—that spirit of movement must be maintained. A problem like this may occur even when you are working

Further Information
☞
Characterization, p.30
Cel, p.52
Backgrounds, p.46

KEEPING A UNITY OF VISION
Making animated films is commonly a team activity. The efforts of everyone in the team must be directed toward bringing the original concept to the screen undiminished. It is easy for inconsistencies to be introduced.

▼ Here we see some of the ways in which the drawing of a character can be changed during animation, due to neglect of detail or inattention to proportion.

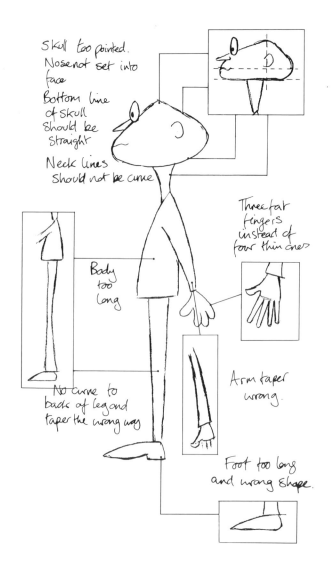

Skull too pointed.
Nose not set into face
Bottom line of skull should be straight
Neck lines should not be curved

Three fat fingers instead of four thin ones

Body too long

Arm taper wrong.

No curve to back of leg and taper the wrong way

Foot too long and wrong shape.

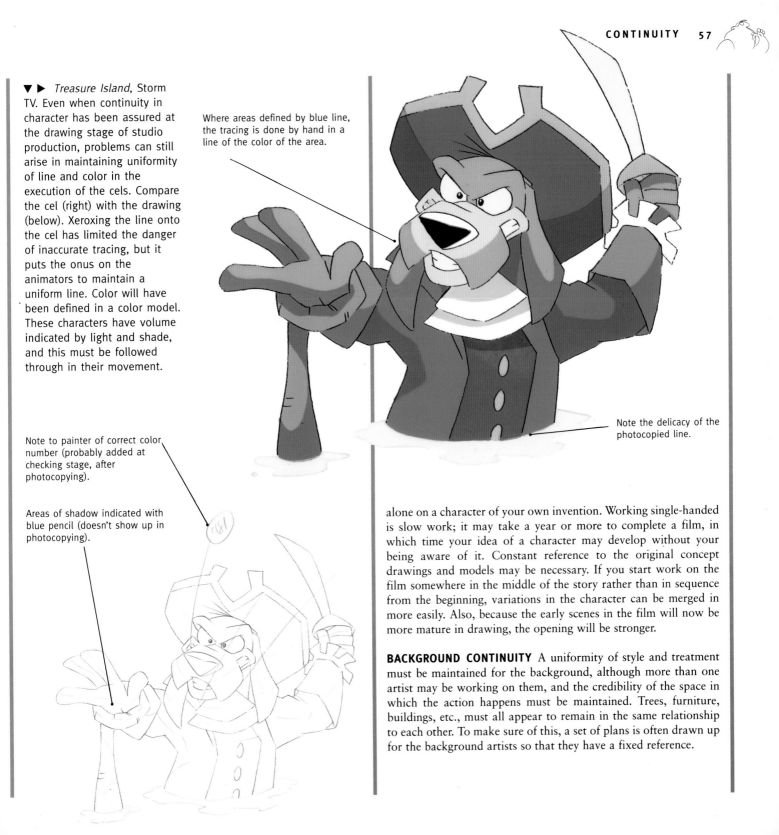

▼ ▶ *Treasure Island*, Storm TV. Even when continuity in character has been assured at the drawing stage of studio production, problems can still arise in maintaining uniformity of line and color in the execution of the cels. Compare the cel (right) with the drawing (below). Xeroxing the line onto the cel has limited the danger of inaccurate tracing, but it puts the onus on the animators to maintain a uniform line. Color will have been defined in a color model. These characters have volume indicated by light and shade, and this must be followed through in their movement.

Where areas defined by blue line, the tracing is done by hand in a line of the color of the area.

Note the delicacy of the photocopied line.

Note to painter of correct color number (probably added at checking stage, after photocopying).

Areas of shadow indicated with blue pencil (doesn't show up in photocopying).

alone on a character of your own invention. Working single-handed is slow work; it may take a year or more to complete a film, in which time your idea of a character may develop without your being aware of it. Constant reference to the original concept drawings and models may be necessary. If you start work on the film somewhere in the middle of the story rather than in sequence from the beginning, variations in the character can be merged in more easily. Also, because the early scenes in the film will now be more mature in drawing, the opening will be stronger.

BACKGROUND CONTINUITY A uniformity of style and treatment must be maintained for the background, although more than one artist may be working on them, and the credibility of the space in which the action happens must be maintained. Trees, furniture, buildings, etc., must all appear to remain in the same relationship to each other. To make sure of this, a set of plans is often drawn up for the background artists so that they have a fixed reference.

Cutout Animation

Cutout animation is the simplest way of using drawings to create action. Being largely an impromptu technique, it is primarily a solo activity.

Cutout work, where the action of animating is done directly under the camera, carries a high personal charge. It is in a sense miming, since the animator is using only his or her judgment and experience to achieve the action. The great master of cutout, Youri Norshtein, was once asked to what extent he used electronic controls on the special rostrum he had made for himself. He rejected them completely, and to explain why, he made an eloquent gesture, tapping his forehead and running his finger from there down his own arm to his hand.

This direct connection between brain and hand is the spirit of cut-out animation. There are two other advantages for a solo animator. First, you need many fewer drawings; the pieces that make up a single figure can be used to create movement that might require hundreds of drawings and cels. Second, the cut-out pieces are likely to be designed and made by the animators themselves.

The range of subject is almost as wide as for any animation technique, stretching from robust gag-based action to something as delicate and sophisticated as Norshtein's *Tale of Tales*. It is true that there are limitations. Fluid movement, particularly in perspective, is not easy to achieve with flat puppets, and cutout will not usually sustain lengths of more than five minutes. Close-ups of faces don't work well, which makes dialogue requiring lip-sync less common, though it is achievable. A mimed story is most typical.

CHARACTERISTICS OF CUTOUT Even if you take great care manipulating the cutouts, the control of movement will never be as fine as it is in full cel animation, and the action should be planned with that in mind. Firm, rapid movement with judicious pauses is the characteristic of cutout. It also lends itself to frantic, chaotic, continuous action, where the vagaries of some of the pieces can be absorbed in the confusion.

Further Information 👉
Rostrum camerawork, p.26
Movement, p.34

▲ A simple cutout character. Large scale for the close-up.

▼ Character made from separate head, body, arm, and leg pieces. The arms are jointed.

▲ Set of interchangeable profile and three-quarter heads for expression changes for the character, left. You can plan the action so that the character may never have to have heads facing the other way.

SIMPLE CUTOUTS

The simplest figures to make and use are silhouettes made from thin black paper. These were not pre-drawn, but cut directly with a knife, using Ingres paper, which is thin and completely opaque.

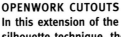

1 Cutting shapes directly with a scalpel.

OPENWORK CUTOUTS

In this extension of the silhouette technique, the paper is cut within the main shapes to give a woodcut effect similar to traditional Chinese paper-cuts. The disadvantage is that these openwork pieces have to be backed with paper of the same material as the ground color to avoid problems when arms cross the body or the figure passes across something else—either another figure or a part of the background scene.

▶ Cutting an open-work head. This gives an opportunity for more decorative detail than plain silhouette.

2 Simple cutouts can be flipped over, using both sides so that the same profile head, or arms and legs, can be used facing either left or right. A film with black silhouette figures is clearly capable of only a limited color range. Black on white, the obvious one, can be extremely effective

for some purposes. It is possible to use other ground colors, but they have to be on the light side, and the background elements used to indicate a scene must be kept to a minimum so they do not conflict with the outline of the character.

▶▼ Backing paper shaped to provide filling for the open shape and avoid confusion with the background.

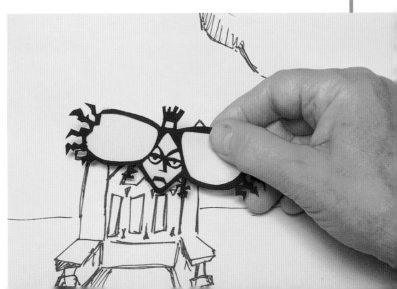

JOINTING

It is possible to work with all the pieces free and separate, but they are easier to manage without jitter in the movement if the limbs are jointed. Here there is a full set of pivot joints including jaw. Complete figures have to be made for left and right profiles and for any changes in hand or foot aspect.

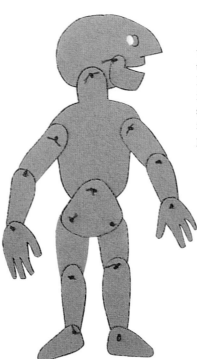

▲ ▶ The thread for the joint is tied into a knot large enough to prevent it from pulling through the base.

There are two things to try to avoid. One is water animation, where a sea or river occupies a large part of the frame. Unless it is to be represented as static, water requires constant animation, at least every other frame, and since it is going to be merely the setting for the main action, it brings an unrealistic burden of labor for a secondary item. The other problem area is bird flight, which also requires perpetual movement as well as three dimensions; without perspective, this animation will soon become tedious.

▼ The finished puppet, with the finishing knots on the underside, is capable of movement limited to the silhouette of the figure.

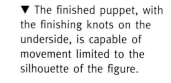

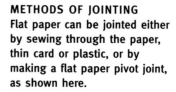

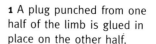

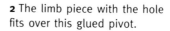

METHODS OF JOINTING

Flat paper can be jointed either by sewing through the paper, thin card or plastic, or by making a flat paper pivot joint, as shown here.

1 A plug punched from one half of the limb is glued in place on the other half.

2 The limb piece with the hole fits over this glued pivot.

3 A small piece of paper is glued to the pivot to prevent the pieces from coming apart. The pieces now rotate freely.

1   2   3   4   5

LIMITATIONS OF JOINTING
With a fully jointed figure, it would be impossible to soften the transition from position 1 to position 5. By keeping the elements loose you can create a form of in-betweening.

▲ In (2) the right arm is brought in front of the body to suggest a turn of the torso, and the eyes begin to move as a lead to the movement. In (3) the left leg piece is changed for a bent leg, and the right arm comes further around. In (4) the direction of the right leg is reversed and a new profile introduced. This prepares for the substitution of the side-on body to complete the action on (5).

MANIPULATING CUTOUTS
Since fingers tend to be both clammy and relatively clumsy, tweezers are the ideal tool. Two pairs of tweezers are best, as you can use one to hold down the bits you want to stay still, and with the other you can push or pull the moving piece.

◀ With a small number of basic elements, an illusion of three-dimensional movement can be created.

WEAR AND TEAR
Paper is naturally fragile, and constant use of tweezers and adhesive can make the pieces look very tired. One way to prolong the life of colored-paper pieces is to cover both front and back surfaces with transparent adhesive film. This protects the color and design of the front, and gives a back surface to which you can apply and remove adhesives such as tape without damaging the paper. You can draw on the plastic-covered front surface to add further features, and if you use wax pencils the additions can be wiped off afterwards.

▲ A patch of self-adhesive film is applied to the cutout piece, smoothed down as the backing paper is withdrawn. The adhesive film is burnished to avoid bubbles and then trimmed to the shape of the piece. Eyes and mouth expressions can now be added, and altered, with wax pencil.

ANIMATING WITH CUTOUTS The rostrum set-up for cutout is the same as that for cel animation, the only small variation being in the use of the pressure glass. In some cases cutout animation does not need a glass over the artwork, but the heat of the lights may cause papers to curl, and cast irritating shadows. Usually some form of glass is desirable, but it may be a loose glass rather than the fixed platen of the standard rostrum. As with drawn animation, concern is to move only those things that are to be moved, and a screen full of pieces of dismembered paper—supposing that there are several characters moving at once—clearly presents some problems. There are various solutions.

One is to separate the characters with layers of cel, but even so you will have to remove and replace the upper layers to move the underneath pieces.

You can stick down the pieces, using either adhesive spray or double-sided tape to attach the static parts of a character to a cel level, and trust to luck with the loose parts. The disturbance caused by pulling a firmly stuck piece off when the time comes to move it may, however, be greater than desirable.

Jointing is another method, though what this gives in control of a figure's constituents is offset by the limitations it brings.

Magnets are sometimes used. Of the various magnetized boards available, the simplest to adapt for cutout animation is a sheet of magnetized rubber—a piece of stiff rubber about ¼-inch thick which has been impregnated with a magnetic oxide. The sheet is laid on the rostrum table, and the background with a protective cel is laid over it. A small piece of ¼-inch recording tape—itself a magnetized substance—can be taped to the back of each cutout piece. Thin iron foil is better, if you can get it, but aluminum foil is no good. The pull of the magnetic rubber, while very strong in direct contact with pure metal, is modified by the intervening layers of paper and cel, and exerts only a weak pull on the cutout. It is enough to stop the paper cutouts flying about too freely, but not so strong as to make it a disrupting effort to move them.

For almost all cutout work it is desirable to put a cel level over the background to protect it while handling the figures. If the background is to move for a panning effect while the characters walk on the spot, a cel which remains static above the background is essential.

FULL COLORED CUTOUTS
These have one immediately obvious advantage over drawn and cel animation. Since the character design does not have to be repeated many times by many hands, a more lavish use of texture, shading, and detail is possible. Cutout figures made of collages of gorgeous patterned papers counterbalance the limitation of movement of which they are capable.

▲ What your character is going to do is the consideration which guides what cutout pieces you will need. These are the basic necessities. Additional pieces you may need are gripping or gesturing hands, bent arms, and three-quarter-view heads. Heads with particular facial expressions may also be a requirement.

CONTROLLING MOVES

Judging the distance to move pieces is something that you must learn by experience. In order to control moves, however, it is sometimes useful to have a piece of paper calibrated with the distance, frame by frame, that you have calculated is the required move.

▲ A calibration is used to calculate the distance the slipping foot moves back for a walk on the spot. If there is a background, the calibration should be paralleled in the background move. The scale is laid in place for the move, but taken away for shooting.

▶ Similar calibrations can be used to guide the speed of other movements.

CUTOUT MOVEMENT STYLE

Even with a limited set of pieces, some lively poses can be obtained. Explosive changes from one pose to another are suggested rather than slow, smooth movement.

◀▶ Probably none of the poses will stand scrutiny for long pauses on the screen, unless you can achieve a really elegant assembly. Quick-fire slapstick is the natural mode.

Drawing on Film

This is the most direct way of creating moving images on film. Animation produced in this way is crude, but has a vigor and freshness that make it effective.

Little equipment is needed, but the variety of images you can create is limited, and because you are working on a very small scale, you cannot achieve much in the way of fine detail. In addition, the placing of images in the frame is largely a matter of guesswork, so precise control of the movement is tricky. The larger the format of the film, the easier it is to limit the difficulties. Thus, 35mm is better than 16mm, but both the stock itself and the final processing are more expensive. The lengths of film on which you work are too fragile to be projected—the drawing would quickly rub off—so it is customary to "bi-pack" the original to get an internegative. The film on which you have scratched or drawn and then colored is passed through the camera gate with unexposed color stock, frame by frame. The backlit panel on the rostrum provides the light source which prints the drawn image onto the unexposed stock, recreating your animation as a negative. This, when developed, can be used to make prints identical to your original work.

MAKING THE DRAWINGS Broadly, there are two kinds of film stock you can use—black or clear. Film that has been exposed but not processed carries a black emulsion coating in which you can scribe marks; these will initially be white, but you can tint them later. Clear film stock, which can be obtained from laboratories, has had all emulsion washed off and has virtually no tone. You can draw on it with a fine pen, use colored inks and dyes, or even apply adhesive lettering and texture. Almost anything can be collaged onto the film, provided it is first small enough, and second can pass through the camera gate without hindrance and without the collaged material falling off.

The film stock you use will probably have no frame lines on it to define the frame, so you will need to count the sprocket holes. With 16mm, there is only one set at the corners of each frame, so it is fairly easy to be sure where your frame is. In the case of 35mm, each frame has four holes at each side, so you have to count carefully. People who work direct on film usually make a small rig to guide the film through and to locate it frame by frame (see illustration opposite). In this way you can to some extent guide the

CREATIVE APPROACHES
Narrative action and comic gags are not easy to achieve in this medium. Its power lies in the cumulative effect of brief, brilliant images.

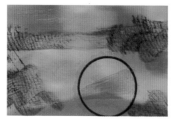 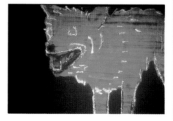

▲ Kayla Parker, *Sunset Strip.* On clear film, brilliant color can be brushed or stained on the film with inks and dyes, and finer images collaged on.

▲ Kayla Parker, *Walking Out.* Scratching the coating of the film is the best way of getting a line drawing onto the frames of film. By coloring both sides of the film, you can color the scratching.

MAKING A RIG
To make a quick way of laying film down in register over your guide drawing, make a rig with register pins to go through the sprocket holes.

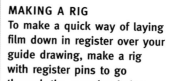

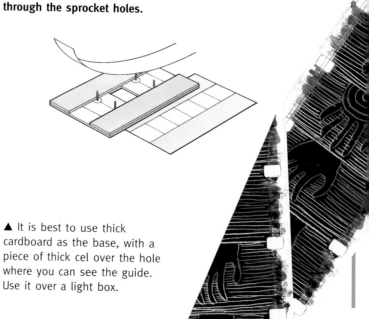

▲ It is best to use thick cardboard as the base, with a piece of thick cel over the hole where you can see the guide. Use it over a light box.

▼ These frames are from Kayla Parker's film *Metamorphosis,* worked on 16mm film. The black image has been drawn on one side of the film, while the color has been either stippled or striped on the other.

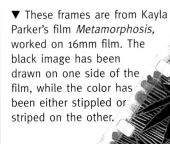

▲ Two further examples from Kayla Parker's work showing the brilliance of color and the line quality which can be achieved.

MAKING A PERMANENT PRINT

The dyes, inks, and transfers on your film are fragile, so some form of internegative must be made from the original. This is done either in a laboratory or by the bipack process, where the drawn-on film and raw stock are passed through the gate of the rostrum camera.

▲ The double bipack is loaded, and the unexposed film and your original pass through the gate together.

movement of shapes within the frame. To control the speed as well, you will need to plan how many frames the movement you have in mind will take, mark the first and last positions the correct number of frames apart, and then add the in-between markings.

ANIMATION STYLE Because of the directness of the photographic process, the colors can be very brilliant, and the textures produced by inks or felt pen on the film can be pleasing. Although fine detail is not easy to achieve, the accidental "burr" occurring at the edge of a scratch in the emulsion can give a "tracery" effect.

Figure animation can only be very broadly treated; this is a style which works best with abstract shapes and is ideal as a direct reflection of a musical soundtrack. The Canadian Norman McLaren's work (in particular, *Vertical Lines*) is a good example of this use.

Mixed Media

Because animated filmmakers are completely in command of their material, they are at liberty to select and use images from any source.

The mixing of methods is almost as old as the movies. George Méliès in the 1900s employed all kinds of ways of making images, with live-shot actors—shot either stop-frame or running camera—joined in the same frame with models and drawings. He regarded this as a natural way of exploiting the film camera. In time, however, animated cartoon drawings dominated commercial film theatrical presentation and were consequently the form most familiar to the public. Any reversion to combining cartoon drawing with other visual tricks was regarded as mixing an alien strand into the standard form of the medium.

Among the most familiar examples of these mixed-media tricks are Mickey Mouse shaking hands with Leopold Stowowski in *Fantasia* and Gene Kelly dancing with Tom and Jerry in *Anchors Aweigh*. Together with other sequences in Disney films (*The Reluctant Dragon, Make Mine Music, Song of the South*), they were interpolations of mixed-image sequences into films that were otherwise either all animation or all live-shot.

With *Who Framed Roger Rabbit* in 1991, a complete feature film was conceived in which live actors and drawn characters interacted fully throughout. This film was based on a script written in the 1950s and probably had to wait until the recent developments in digital effects could overcome the problems of giving real unity to the cartoon and live elements. The subtleties of natural lighting are usually at odds with the uniform tone of flat drawn animation, but in *Roger Rabbit*, great care was taken to give the correct light and shade modeling on the cartoon figures. Then their blending with the live-shot actors and scenery was governed digitally so that the fine variations of lighting were the same for both sets of images.

Futuristic films such as *Terminator* and *Robocop* could also be called mixed media, in the sense that the principal characters are combined with so many special effects that you can never be sure whether it is an actor, a model, or a computer-generated image that represents a character. Computer equipment capable of manipulating and combining images from many sources are becoming ever-cheaper, and complicated effects which were once only possible for

DIFFERENT APPROACHES
Who Framed Roger Rabbit, animation by Richard Williams, produced by Steven Spielberg—a big budget, no-expense-spared production. *Picnic*, Speedy Films, Paul Vester, was produced on a comparatively small budget.

▲ Every frame was treated digitally to blend the lighting of the animation tonally with the live material.

▼ This is cel animation using photographs rather than painted backgrounds. The film needed direct photographic realism to emphasize its social comment.

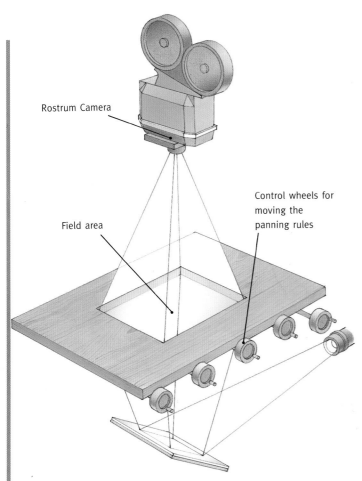

Rostrum Camera

Control wheels for
moving the
panning rules

Field area

AERIAL IMAGE ROSTRUM
The back-lit panel of the
rostrum means the projected
live action can be focused
directly into the camera lens
while the animation cels
appear as a black silhouette.

▲ After shooting once, the
animation cels are lit from
above against black. The
scene is then reshot, this
time filling in the color of
the animation while the
black background does not
interfere with the exposed
live action.

comment, and tends to be associated with jazzy quick cutting. It is hard to imagine its being sustainable beyond two or three minutes, which also makes it suitable for music videos.

COMBINING ANIMATION AND LIVE ACTION By the traditional method, combining the two in the same frame of film involves several stages and optical printing in a laboratory. It is possible to circumvent that process by using what is called an "aerial image" rostrum which replaces some of the laboratory stages (see illustration.)

With the current use of videotape, the combining is even easier. Full-color animation is shot (either on video or on film transferred to video) on a primary-color background, usually blue. This can easily be combined with any other video image by video editing. The process is generally known as "blue screen." Matching, positioning, and synchronization are, to some extent, also capable of adjustment at this editing stage.

COMBINING PUPPETS AND LIVE FILM This can be achieved by the process known as front light/back light, which is roughly similar to the aerial image process described. But there are other ways of combining step-frame object or puppet animation with live action.

The actors can themselves be shot stop-frame (this is called pixillation) at the same time as the animation of the puppets, as in *Tom Thumb* by Dave Borthwick, or, as with Jan Svankmajer's *Food*, by simply intercutting the live actors with puppets which replace them. The puppets can do those actions which are impossible in reality. The film flows continuously, and no attempt is made to disguise the transitions from live-shot to animation.

CARTOON ANIMATION ON STILL PHOTOGRAPHS Obviously the use of photographs as a background poses no particular technical problems. It is also possible to shoot animation on photographic backgrounds that involve movement. There is a process by which the frames of live action can be printed out, registered to the right size for the animating frame. Thus cartoon figures can be followed through a moving background without extra technical processes. The quality of the prints is good, but perhaps not as good as the optical printing process, so it is more useful as a background location in animation.

CUT-OUT WITH PHOTOGRAPHS AND DRAWINGS Technically this is the same as ordinary cut-out. The main purpose is to use the contrast, even absurdity, of the mixture of elements.

big-budget movies will become normal. Our acceptance of such mixtures will go hand in hand with that.

Properly, however, the term "mixed media" should only apply to films which make us aware of the mixing of two kinds of images, with the filmmaker intending an uneasy blend of the two. Mixing drawings and photographs as a collage, frame by frame, is the most recognizable form and needs no special technical process. For some reason, this kind of combined image lends itself to satire and social

Sand and Glass

In both these techniques, images are made in a fluid substance on a backlit or bright surface. The marks made remain long enough to be filmed, but can be changed for the next move.

Unlike the drawn lines of conventional animation, the pictures are created in areas of light and shade by scribing or brushing into the paint or sand. When paint is used, the images can be fully colored, but with sand it is usually monochrome.

The movement of the animation is created by gradually modifying the drawing, frame by frame. Sand retains its fluidity, of course, but paint must be kept moist. Oil paint, which is slow-drying, is the best medium; the same scene can be worked on for several days without the paint's drying up, even on a lightbox, provided it is covered with a damp cloth when it is to be left for any time (for an example of this technique, see page 108).

As with cutouts, the work is done directly under the camera, so the techniques are well suited to the solo filmmaker. Because it is impromptu work, you need to be confident of your drawing skills, and of course you must have unlimited access to a rostrum camera, as the whole of the animation is created there.

Both techniques work best on glass, but a glass surface is not essential for sand. For the painted method, glass has to be used, as it provides a nonabsorbent surface which can be wiped clean of paint as necessary. A light box beneath the glass makes the work much easier, but it is not absolutely necessary. For either technique, one of the useful things about the glass is that pre-drawn key positions can be slipped under it as guides for the movement. When sand is animated over a light, it produces a highly contrasted light and dark image, which can be shot on black-and-white film. If the image is reversed—positive to negative—areas which were black or dark become light, and vice versa; white shapes on a dark ground become dark shapes on white.

> **Further Information**
> ☞
> Rostrum camerawork, p.26
> Cutout animation, p.58

ANIMATING WITH SAND
Animating with sand or paint on glass can be done freely without any predrawn guidance, but it is an advantage to have a method such as that shown here, where preliminary layouts can be used.

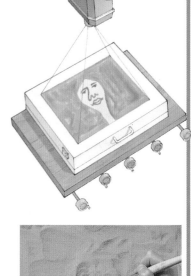

▶ Although this work is normally done by placing a box on the usual rostrum table, any horizontal surface with a downward-pointing camera will serve.

▼ ▶ Using the reference drawing, the first image is made in the sand using fingers and a brush to define the shapes and create textures in the sand.

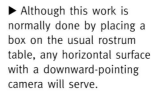

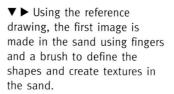

1   Once the frame is complete, the reference drawing is removed and the shot taken. (The backlit effect is shown inset.)

2   A general view of the set-up. The specially designed glass tray is placed on the rostrum table over a back light.

Besides your fingers, brushes and wooden skewers are useful tools for moving the sand. Stencils can serve to define shapes, particularly for background details. If the work is top-lit, textures can be created by pressing objects into the sand. A small strainer is a useful way of adding a fine layer of sand to shade areas.

3   The first in an action series. In-between positions have been omitted.

4   By shifting the sand around, a new pose has been achieved, step by step.

5   The hand has now been moved down, leaving the spoon.

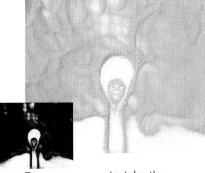

6   A stage in the metamorphosis of the image. The figure is shrinking as the spoon moves up ...

7   ... to take the principal role ...

8   ... and turn back to the original image.

Animation With a Computer

Perhaps the best way to approach the subject is to think first of the earliest use of computers in animation production, which was to provide the rostrum camera with digital control.

Since all the movements and controls of the rostrum were mathematically calibrated, it was a simple matter to replace the fallibility of hand and memory with a digital program controlling the sequence of actions required to shoot frame by frame. It greatly increased the potential of rostrum shooting to be able to repeat precisely—or vary the movements of the table, the camera, and the shutter, according to a preset program.

This did not mean though, that an untutored person could approach the machine and press a button so that programs inside the computer would do all that was required to shoot the artwork. It still needed the skill and knowledge of an experienced rostrum operator to use the programs that controlled it to the best advantage. The approach to animation drawn through, or assisted by, a computer, must be the same. Only if you are thoroughly conversant with all animation techniques—those of layout, design, movement, and timing, not to mention editing and sound—can you expect to use a computer as a tool to produce good animation.

With this warning in mind, we can also say that the programs available for computer animation do offer a vast selection of possibilities to a knowledgeable operator. So vast, in fact, that there is a danger of being tempted by the things the computer can do, rather than using its abilities to achieve what you want.

Before we go deeper into the possibilities of computer technology, it maybe helpful to establish another proviso. The quality of both the image and the animation produced via a computer is in direct ratio to the computing power, and consequently the cost, of the hardware and programs. There are three drawbacks in working with the cheaper end of the line. They are slowness of rendering each frame, coarseness of line and shape definition, and capacity of memory in terms of the number of frames that can be stored.

▲ *Ray tracing* is the name for the computer programs which provide flawless lighting effects to the apparent surfaces of computer generated images. The artist can select the position of a light source, the nature of the light (diffused, spot, brilliant, etc) and the reflectivity of the surfaces lit. Any action performed by the shapes will occur within this lighting environment. Ray tracing is commonly used for spectacular shiny juggling of this kind. This image was created by Raytech BBS.

▶ *The Wrong Brothers*, Steve Weston, Whitehorse Films/Bermuda Shorts. Here the control of lighting available to the computer animator has been used to more subtle, not to say humane, effect. Each surface texture has a separate response to the assumed overhead sunlight. This is animation through a computer, by an animator with considerable experience of traditional methods. It is true character animation in the cartoon tradition, but affected by the bias of all computer work toward "reality."

◀ *Coiled Golden Mutation*, William Latham. This is the work of an artist who prefers pure mathematics to the creation of illusory images either naturalistic or abstract. His animated sequences are the product of a sort of breeding process achieved by the "mating" of mathematical concepts to breed other forms.

2-D SYSTEMS These are programs which give the opportunity to manipulate flat areas. Because they work well for animation drawings with limited movement, but offer a wide choice of ways in which those drawings can be utilized, they are frequently used in television-series production.

These programs eliminate many of the production stages and assist greatly with others. Even where the original animation drawing is hand-done and scanned into the computer's system, all manual tracing and coloring is eliminated, the drawings are available for all kinds of manipulation and repetition, and the recording and tabulation required in organizing production are taken care of. Drawings created directly on the computer screen can be similarly handled.

There are programs which allow you to file drawings in such a way that they can be called up in any order, re-used in other scenes, reduced or magnified, and all recorded and tabulated on a dope sheet which can either be displayed on the screen or printed out. An almost infinite number of levels of animation can be handled

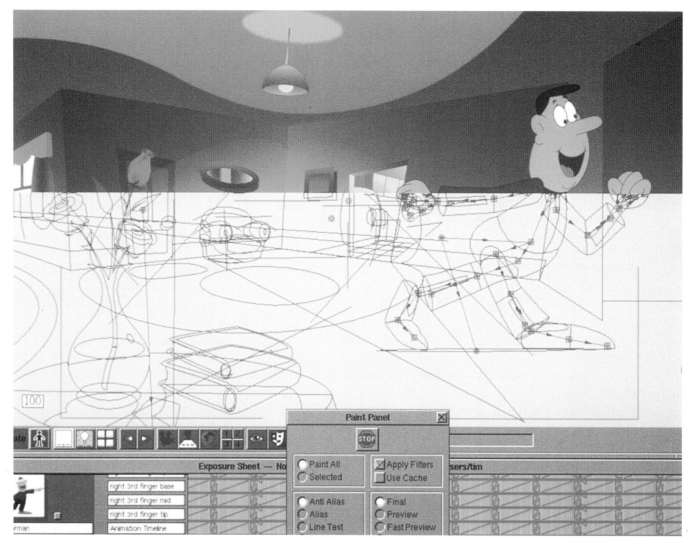

2-D SYSTEMS
The value of the computer to animation production, even with the limitation of only two-dimensional movement, is that it is not only a substitute for laborious hand coloring. Some in-between movements are possible, and the computing power of the machine can simplify production control and scheduling.

▲ ▶ Two illustrations of Animo, the Cambridge Animation System. Above, the character shape is altered by shifting key points. Right, the relationship between the basic geometry and the final rendered image. The menu indicates how all the production processes are contained in the programs.

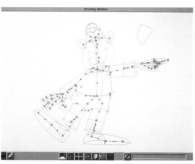

THE SOLO ANIMATOR

The 2-D computer is useful not only to assist mass production. The following is an account by Ruth Lingford of the way she uses a computer to make personal films.

"For me, the main advantage of using the computer is the instant feedback it gives me on my animation. The techniques I use are not particularly quick, but the coloring process is much easier with the computer. I work on Amiga computers, and have mainly used two distinct methods, both using the Deluxe Paint VI program. For me, drawing is infinitely easier with a digitizing tablet and pen—some people can draw very well using a mouse, but I find it extremely difficult."

(unlike the limitations of cel levels), and camera movements can be programmed in. Computers also have an audio system so that the sound track can be recorded and analyzed in the computer, and there are programs which will relate predesigned mouth movements for the characters directly to the audio track.

The effect of all this is to change the approach to animation. Instead of preplanning the timing of actions by spacing the key poses and then drawing the in-betweens to test the movement, the animator working with a computer will be likely to feed the single-pose drawings into the system and then use the computer program to space them and determine the number of in-betweens. The freedom to try out a variety of possible timings without prior

1 As in traditional animation, the animator starts with a line drawing, then uses the Light Table facility for tracing, to draw first key drawings, then in-betweens. She then goes back and colors the frames, going over each line twice to soften and vary the over-uniform lines. She can play back at any time to check the movement, and can add or subtract frames easily.

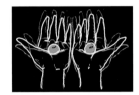
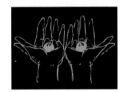

2 This is a technique similar to painting on glass. The animator first creates a line test of the movement using the Light Table. Using the first frame, she then draws the finished look of the animation, using blocks of color, textures, detail, etc. She adds an identical frame and modifies it by adding and subtracting, flicking to the next frame of the line test for a guide to the movement. She copies this second frame over the next frame of line test and changes it again, again flicking forward to the next frame for reference. When the piece of animation is complete, she saves it on the PAR (Personal Animation Recorder), which can run quite long pieces of animation to accurate time, and then transfers from there to broadcast-quality video. For festival screenings, the animator transfers to 16mm film from the video.

calculation may, in the end, damage your ability to judge what is best, however. Too much choice can be dangerous.

COLORING BY COMPUTER Even relatively simple programs will offer a considerable choice of colors with which to color line drawings, while the more elaborate ones offer mind-boggling numbers of color possibilities. Putting the selected color onto the character or object animated is done by simply moving the cursor to the area you have defined. In general, this has to be an unbroken enclosing line. Colors can be changed at will to try out different combinations. Shading and texture, hard to control on hand-colored cels, can be added, as well as various effects such as ripple glass, focus pulling, backlight, pixie-dust, and glows. Some programs allow you to alter the opacity of the color to get transparent areas. Provided you take account of changes in aspect of the figure during movement—turning around to show previously unseen detail, for example—the coloring of one drawing of the character can be extended to all the others in the sequence by a touch of a switch. Even at a late stage in production, you can change your mind about coloring. Such changes are automatically transmitted to all the drawings scene by scene.

With this sort of animation production, there are no hard-and-fast divisions between traditional hand-drawn and computer-assisted methods. In some cases, all except the final coloring of figure and background may be done on paper, while in others, almost all the animation may also be computer-generated.

3-D SYSTEMS Whereas the simpler 2-D programs give the illusion of movement by manipulating flat areas, the 3-D systems operate by manipulating volume through genuine three-dimensional movements. Basic geometric shapes of cubes, cylinders, and spheres are used to construct moveable characters. The programs available vary in sophistication, but, broadly, under your control they will change, turn, and move whatever three-dimensional shape you design, according to set rules. For figure animation, joint movement can be programmed so that only what is natural for limbs can be animated. At the very highest level, on expensive computers with expensive programs, the choice of possibilities open to a creative animator seem dazzlingly infinite.

RECORDING THE IMAGE Whatever computer or program you have, the animation you create has to be transferred to another element in order to be shown to a viewer or an audience. For video, transfer to digital tape is common, but for theatrical release, the image from the original digital disk has to be put through a film recorder to create a negative from which prints are made. The interaction between film and digital tape is now highly developed. As in the whole of computer development, the best advances are made by combining the advantages of old and new technology.

3-D SYSTEMS IN ACTION
Once the animator has a clear and precise idea of what the action is to be, the steps in creating animation with a 3-D program are as follows:

1 Character built in wire frame using patch modeling.

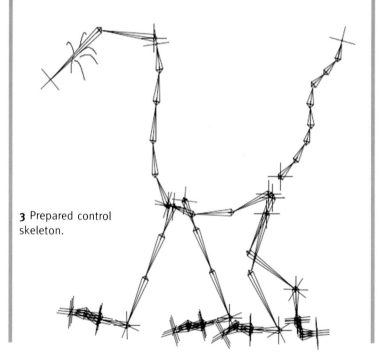

2 Completed character model.

3 Prepared control skeleton.

4 Finished model with skeleton assigned.

5 Characters animated in partial set having established camera position.

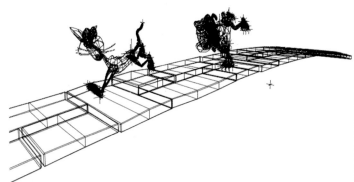

6 Set built in wire frame using polygonal modeling.

Model Animation

The spirit which inspires puppet or model animators seems to be a different one from that which drives drawn ones. Although there are exceptions, it is uncommon for those skilled in the one field to cross over to the other or to create in both fields.

Historically, the explanation for the divide is a simple one. Drawn animation grew out of the comic strip and comic book, allied to vaudeville performance. These forms were native to the United States, and the first commercial production of cartoon films developed in U.S. studios. When the full power of American industrial know-how was applied to the system, the preeminence of drawn animation was assured by the dominance of the American product.

Puppet animation, on the other hand, grew out of a European tradition and has remained largely so. The existence of a long history of puppet theater in eastern and southern Europe meant that as people discovered the power of stop-motion, it was natural to work with puppets. A similar tradition existed in Japan, and puppet animation flourishes there. These regional divisions have been blurred over the last 30 years, but the popularity of puppet or object animation outside the United States continues.

Artistically, the appeal to an audience of the two media is much the same. From the creator's point of view, the elements with which puppet animators work is less flexible. Characters and scenery, once built, are not so easily adapted and transformed. There is the practical benefit, though that, with these materials in hand, making a film involves less tedious repetitive work than drawn animation.

Munk and Lemmy—Let's Fly, The Animacijas Brigada. A typical example of the puppet genre from Eastern Europe. The most copious and celebrated producers of such material were the Czechs, where stop-frame puppet work seemed to be a major

Tools and Equipment

The first requirement for a model animator is space. Because you are working in three dimensions, you need a set with lighting and the space to move a camera around it.

Besides the shooting area, model animation requires a workshop, or at least a workbench, on which to build both the puppets and sets; animation of this kind is really live-action filmmaking in miniature. This is not to say that an enormous hangar must be found before you can think of starting. It is possible to work in quite a small spare room, or in an empty garage—a practical minimum would be 10 square feet.

BASIC TOOLS
You would expect to work with wire, wood, plaster, latex, and clay, and to use the ordinary tools needed to work with these materials.

1 Tape measure; **2** and **4** Scissors for making clothes for puppets; **3** Pliers for wire; **5** Wire for armatures; **6** Plaster; **7** Latex; **8** Thread for sewing; **9** Pins for securing puppets' feet; **10** Modeling clay; **11** Hammers for set-making; **12** Soldering iron for wire, etc.

CAMERA AND LIGHTS Any kind of film or video camera can be used, provided it has a single-framing capacity. The same kind of stop-frame controls for video recording that are used for drawn animation are equally suitable for 3-D work. (Often a simple computer-based recorder is used alongside the film camera, giving instant playback of the animation to review the movement.) A choice of three or four lenses is desirable, particularly if there is limited space to move the camera; a wide-angle and a zoom lens are obvious choices. Sixteen-mm film cameras with stop-frame capacity are usually driven by windup mechanisms, but can be adapted to take a stop-frame electric motor. This gives the shutter action a more positive drive and eliminates the danger of flicker.

A scratch lighting system using ordinary household lights fitted with spot bulbs and some photo-floods would do for a start. More professional lights with an output of 5-800 watts can be added. For a satisfactory lighting system, it is desirable to have all the lights controlled from a bank of dimmers. This gives greater flexibility and prolongs the life of the bulbs when switching on—bulbs can be an expensive item.

MAKING MODELS The materials for making models or puppets vary depending on the kind you are going to animate. The simplest type, and the simplest material, is modeling clay. There are patent variants which are not affected by the heat of the lights. You will need wire for armatures, which are skeleton structures that give firmness to the figure, and for more complicated puppet figures, limbs of short lengths of rod joined with mechanical joints. Such skeletons are usually covered with latex or a silicon mixture.

Heads are cast in molds made from either modeled clay or carved-wood originals. Plaster of paris is a useful substance for making molds. If your puppets need costumes, sewing materials will obviously be needed, and for anything to do with wood—either for puppets or for building sets—a selection of saws, chisels, hammers, and so on will be needed.

BUILDING SETS Sets are built of cardboard, masonite, and light wooden frames. Balsa wood, because of its lightness and ease of cutting, is frequently used for both puppets and sets, as is the plastic core board used in making architectural models. This is an invaluable material, light but rigid, easy to cut, and with a good surface for drawing or painting on. Haunt your local hobby or model train store, and you will soon pick up some ideas for materials to adapt.

Further Information 🖙
Puppet making, p.82
Sets, p.90

DIFFERENT LENSES

▼ 20mm: this wide-angle lens gives a wide general view from a relatively close camera position. Useful when working in a confined space.

 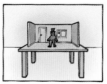

▼ 35mm to 55mm: at the same distance from the subject, this lens gives a general view of the set with deep focus.

▼ 180mm: closer views of the subject from the same camera position. It has a shallow focal plane so that when focused on a foreground object, the background goes soft.

▼ Zoom lens: allows a size variation from normal image up to extreme close-up.

SET-UP FOR MODEL ANIMATION
A well-equipped model animation studio. The scene is set for filming to begin.

1 Lighting gantry suspended from ceiling to leave floor clear. **2** Stable platform for model set. **3** Soft surface to allow feet to be pinned.
4 Film camera (stop-frame).
5 Geared head for turning camera and adjusting its angle. **6** Tripod. **7** Spreader to stabilize tripod.
8 Sandbags to weigh down tripod and spreader. **9** Video camera for recording movement next to film camera for instant playback. **10** Control unit for video recorder.
11 Monitor for viewing instant playback.
12 Distant background.
13 Banks of floodlights for background. **14** Dimmers to control each light.
15 Various tools kept handy.
16 Control of stop-frame motor on film camera.

Characterization

Although this kind of animation usually suggests puppets representing either human or animal characters, it is possible to make a character of any object, even an inanimate one.

As with drawn animation, the characterization lies more in what the character does than in what it looks like. With imagination, a chocolate bar, a bottle, or a simple screw can be turned into the hero or heroine of a drama. The brothers Quay and their mentor, Jan Svankmajer, have produced deeply unsettling films using everyday objects to convey mysterious undertones to the fabric of normal life. In the making of commercials, too, advertising a product will often quite naturally call for animating it—or the package which contains it. Hours of skilled work may go into the construction and moving of a squeezy bottle for 30 seconds.

LIVING CREATURES Where puppets represent humans or animals, much the same rules of design apply as to drawn work. Proportions tend to be similar, emphasizing head, hands, and feet, so that the facial features can be clearly seen and the gestures of the hands made positive. Big feet also have the advantage of giving a puppet a stable support. As with drawn work, the screen proportion favors squat rather than elongated figures, and thin gangly shapes are obviously harder to keep stable.

Because of the difficulties of continuous mouth movement, lip-sync is less used in puppet animation than in drawn work. Mime tends to predominate. Dialogue is possible, though, and some animators, like the Aardman Studio, have specialized in this aspect. The materials the puppets are made from relate to the character of their movement. Modeling clay and similar materials give fluid, boneless movement, and do not lend themselves to finesse in detail, since the material itself must be pushed and pulled for creating facial expressions or finger gestures. Metamorphoses are natural to "claymation," which is the generic term for this kind of work.

A wire armature with a

Further Information ☞
Puppet making, p.82
Making puppets move, p.88

SHAPES AND SIZES
Characters come in all shapes and sizes, from the meticulously lifelike to the baldly abstract.

▶ These characters from the "Gog" series by Aaargh! Animation are typcial examples of concept drawings for comic puppets. Big hands, big feet, big heads.

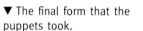
▼ The final form that the puppets took.

A puppet made for a commercial by 3 Peach to promote road safety for children. It was sponsored by McDonald's. The simple shape of the puppet reflects the limited action it is to perform (see the storyboard on p.19).

▼ *Spotless Dominoes* by Philip Hunt. A wire and latex puppet, more abstract than the other examples shown here, and capable because of its construction of considerable fluidity of movement.

silicon or foam latex covering can achieve more definite actions and more sophisticated detail. It does not have the pliability of clay, so facial expressions are more limited. For this sort of puppet, costumes made of cloth or paper are suitable; for animal characters, use fur fabrics of various kinds.

Creating lifelike puppets may be a challenge, but over-realism is not necessarily a suitable aim. In going toward naturalistic appearance, the animator loses two things. Because the creations raise an expectation of verisimilitude, they disappoint by not achieving perfection in terms of the living creature they imitate. And further, the large imaginative scope available to the animator in distortion and particular emphasis, not to speak of making the impossible happen, is lost by following reality too closely.

DEVELOPING A PUPPET CHARACTER It is uncommon for a puppet, once built, to be taken apart and rebuilt, or built a second time with improvements.

Puppet Making

Puppets suitable for frame-by-frame movement can be made from modeling clay, or they can have a skeleton structure, either a flexible wire armature or a rod-and-joint construction.

Characters made of modeling clay or a similar substance are usually made completely, that is, the figure and its clothes are all made of the same material. Because of the pliability of modeling clay, these characters are well suited to broad gag-based animation, since there is more opportunity for distortion or exaggerating the shape than there is with a fixed skeleton.

The flexible wire armature technique is used for puppets which are intended to represent human or animal characters more directly. The body is formed with silicon or latex, and the puppets will probably have costumes made of cloth and leather. The flexibility of the armature gives more opportunity for unnatural movement than jointed rod puppets, but, because the proportions are set by the armature, there is little scope for distortion.

Rod-and-joint puppets are more durable than those with a wire armature; wire eventually breaks with constant bending and straightening. Because the form of the puppets imitates more closely the structure of the humans or animals they represent, they have a more lifelike appearance, with movements that appear naturalistic. The themes and subjects in which such puppets appear thus tend to be dramatic and lyrical rather than outrageous.

GENERAL POINTS There are two extra things to bear in mind when making puppets. First, it is advisable to have small-size versions (about one-fifth of the original) of your puppets so that you can shoot long-distance views without having to go a very long way back or build extensive sets. Second, if you plan a long film, or have more than one animator working, you should have at least two of every principal puppet in case of accidental damage.

Further Information
☞
Making puppets move,
p.88

DEVELOPING A CHARACTER
These are all illustrations of the three stages of making puppet characters – the design, the structure planning, and the finished piece.

▼ ▶ From the "Gogs" series by Aaargh! Animation. Here we have the original visualization and a plan of how the skeleton will be jointed.

▼ Compare this photograph of the finished puppet with the designs.

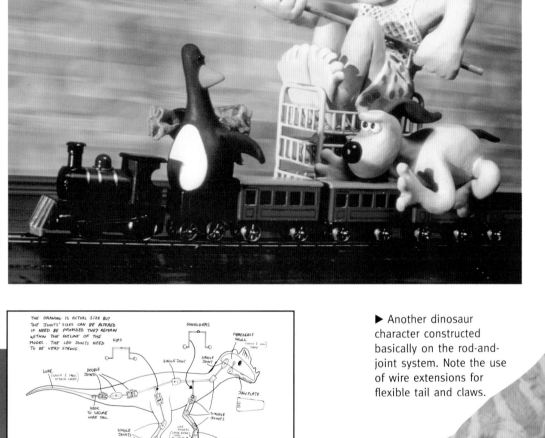

STRUCTURE AND CHARACTER
The structure of a puppet is an important factor in shaping character design.

◄ Wallace and Gromit from *The Wrong Trousers* by Nick Park, Aardman Animation. The lower limbs were a rod jointed skeleton with steel feet so they could be magnetized. The more flexible arms had a wire armature.

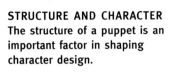

► Another dinosaur character constructed basically on the rod-and-joint system. Note the use of wire extensions for flexible tail and claws.

▲► A similar set of pictures for another character in the series, with details of the joint structure.

CLAY PUPPET WITH A BALSA WOOD AND WIRE ARMATURE

Use aluminum wire which is flexible, does not break easily, and holds its position when bent. Balsa wood and short lengths of tube provide bulk without weight in the rigid sections.

3 Push the wire into holes in the balsa. Join all pieces with strong epoxy glue.

6 Make the fingers from copper wire stuck into the balsa-wood "palms."

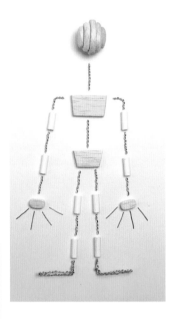

These are the body and limb elements required for the figure. The head is laminated from slices of balsa. The wire is braided for strength.

2 Shape the rounded edges with sandpaper. Then braid the wire to be used for the flexible joints.

4 Join together head, chest, and pelvic sections in this way. Add the wire for the shoulder and thigh joints.

7 Completing the arms and hands.

1 Cut the body and head sections from ½-inch-thick balsa wood.

5 The tubular pieces for the arms and legs are glued onto the wire.

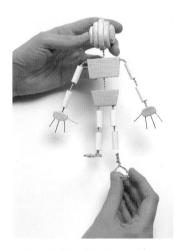

8 Completing the legs with wire armatures for the feet. Make sure the feet are solid enough to take the weight of the upright figure.

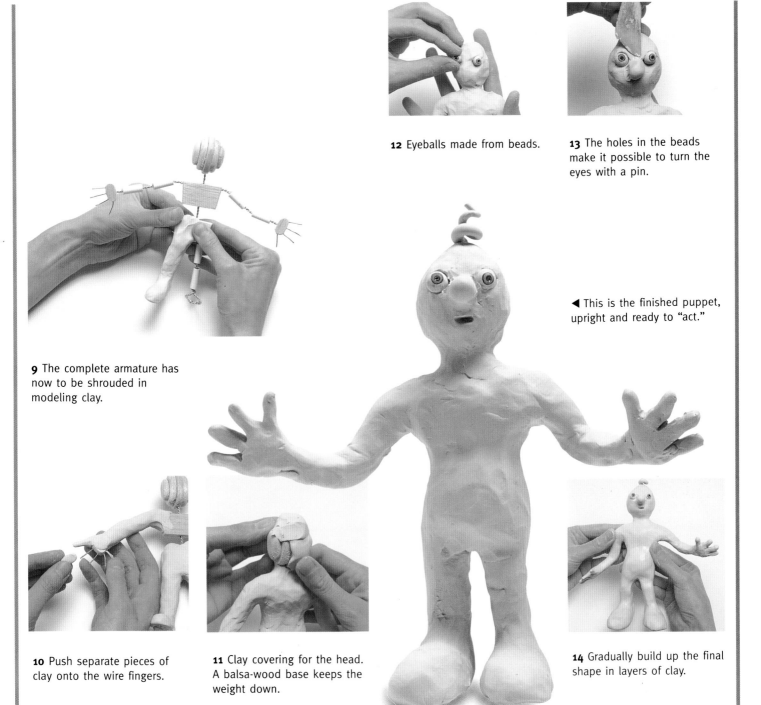

12 Eyeballs made from beads.

13 The holes in the beads make it possible to turn the eyes with a pin.

9 The complete armature has now to be shrouded in modeling clay.

◀ This is the finished puppet, upright and ready to "act."

10 Push separate pieces of clay onto the wire fingers.

11 Clay covering for the head. A balsa-wood base keeps the weight down.

14 Gradually build up the final shape in layers of clay.

A PUPPET WITH BALL-AND-SOCKET JOINTS

To make a more durable puppet with lifelike detail—in this case, a scarecrow character—a more robust armature is required. Ball-and-socket joints can be bought from specialist suppliers, but they can also be made.

5 The hands are finished in foam and painted over a palm and finger base.

6 Loose trousers cover the skeleton legs without any further building for flesh.

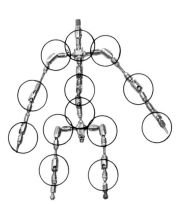

▲ This is the basic assembly of rods and joints. The 13 flexible joints are indicated.

2 The shirt goes straight over the body and arms, showing the straw of the torso.

3 The head has been precast from fiberglass and the bead eyeballs added.

1 Balsa wood or thin foam is put in the places needing solidity. The torso piece already has straw detail attached.

4 Screwing the head onto the neck rod. The neck joint both bends and turns.

7 The boots are made with a joint in the middle to make the feet flexible.

8 The nut which holds the ankle joint is tightened. Here you can see how the ball joint is built.

9 Extra straw stuffing, simulated with paper, is put in place.

10 The figure is flexible enough to have its jacket put on as though in life.

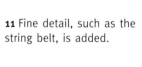

11 Fine detail, such as the string belt, is added.

12 The hat is attached firmly to the rod in the skull.

13 The finished scarecrow.

Making Puppets Move

As in drawn animation, the force and nature of the movement is controlled by the distance moved from frame to frame, but there are two differences in model animation.

The first is that all movement is "straight ahead"—as in animating cutouts, you cannot fix key positions and then make the in-between moves. The second difference is that you cannot control your figure absolutely, making it go wherever you want, as you can with drawn movement, because puppet figures are limited by gravity.

WALKING, JUMPING, AND FLYING Almost all puppets will over-balance if put on one leg—some are hard to keep upright even on two feet. For a walking puppet, you can get around this either by pushing a pin through the foot into whatever substance is used to provide the surface for the action, or by using magnets. If the feet contain a lump of ferrous material, a powerful magnet attached under the working stage will hold the grounded foot in place. Again, there are two solutions to animating a puppet which appears to be in midair. One is to use a sheet of glass sloping away from the camera and attach the puppet to it with self-adhesive tack. When properly lit, the glass is invisible. The other method is invisible supports, which can be either fine nylon threads suspending the puppet, or a horizontal rod support in the back.

As with cutout animation, movement is planned by estimating the number of frames an action will take—the timing—and then breaking the distance to be moved into the size of movement per exposed frame. If you are not confident that a judgment by eye of the distance to be moved is reliable, you can rig a pointer which swings in and out of frame. By setting the pointer against the last position you have a reference for the next move.

Further Information
☞
Cutout animation, p.58
Movement, p.34

GIVING MOVEMENT TO A CLAY FIGURE
Most of the problems to be overcome in moving an upright figure frame by frame are related to its weight. This is particularly true of puppets made of clay, which is a dense material.

▲ ▶ When a figure like this brings its foot forward, the moving foot, which is in mid-air during the action must be supported or the figure will fall. Keeping the support invisible is a problem.

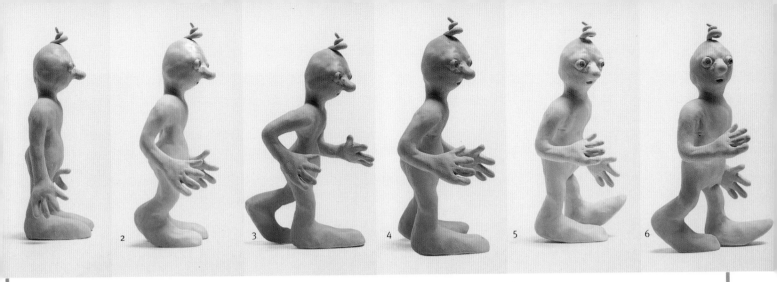

WALKING PACE

A single walking pace at usual speed lasts an average of ½ to ⅔ of a second, or 12 to 16 frames. At two frames a move, that implies 6 or 8 positions. Here we show a 6-position sequence.

▲ From a standing pose (1), the figure moves into the walk (2 and 3) and brings the far foot through for the walk (4, 5, and 6).

▲▼ To keep the figure from overbalancing, a prop can be used, but obviously it must be unobtrusive. Or the static foot can be firmly anchored to the walking surface.

MORPHING

With a pliable substance like clay, it is almost as easy to make progressive transformations as it is in drawing.

▲▶ Starting with a single lump of clay and needing no armature, a series of shape changes can be animated.

Sets

Besides the artistic style of a set, on which animators will have their own ideas, you should bear in mind three practical constraints—camera viewpoint, lighting positions, and accessibility to the puppets.

The scale of the set will relate to the size of your puppets, but both, of course, must be governed by the space you have to work in. You will want to work with pieces as big as is convenient, but there is no point making puppets two feet high which will require equally large sets if your working space is confined. Jan Svankmajer, in *Food*, used life-sized tables, chairs, and food settings in order to be able to switch to live actors from the puppets when he needed to, but since the setting was an ordinary room which he did not have to construct, the scale of the set was not a problem.

The degree of detail and realism you plan as a background to the model animation will obviously depend on the theme of the film. A cozy domestic story such as *The Wind in the Willows* will require a more detailed "real" setting than an abstract symbol of human life such as *Adam* by Peter Lord or *Doors* by David Anderson. In Barry Purves' *Screenplay*, the set is as much part of the story as the characters. The moving screens of a Japanese house are used to further the development of the plot.

SET CONSTRUCTION Whatever the style and size of your set, you will need some specialized materials, or items that can be adopted for the purpose. Useful construction materials are styrofoam board for flat walls and structures; balsa wood, which can be easily carved to represent any wooden object; sponge and plastic foam for trees and bushes (some sprays of evergreen which do not droop quickly are also useful).

Ready-made dolls' furniture and miniature model kits can be adapted to your use. Transparent plastic sheeting makes a credible water surface when stretched, while surgical cotton is good for fog and mist, and papier-mâché spread on chicken wire for rocks. Styrofoam blocks are also useful for rock and can be carved to represent brickwork.

> **Further Information** 👉
> Filming and lighting, p.94

◀▲ These stills from *The Stain* by Marjut Rimminen and Christine Roche are excellent examples of atmospheric domestic interior. The lighting increases the effect, particularly the contrast between the brilliance outside the windows and the gloom inside.

▼ Another home interior from *Rescue Team—the Glue* by the Latvian Studio Animacijas Brigade. All the detail contributes to the feeling of cozy domesticity.

REALISTIC SETS
The examples on these pages are testimony to the way puppet animation requires a degree of realism not so common in drawn animation.

▼ A design for a similar set-up to the one shown below. With the curved backdrop, several camera angles are possible.

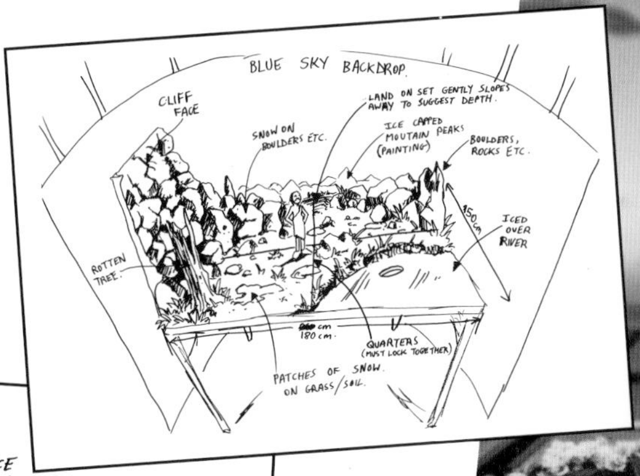

▼ A more limited set-up designed for a single camera position for the "Gogs" series from Aaargh! Animation.

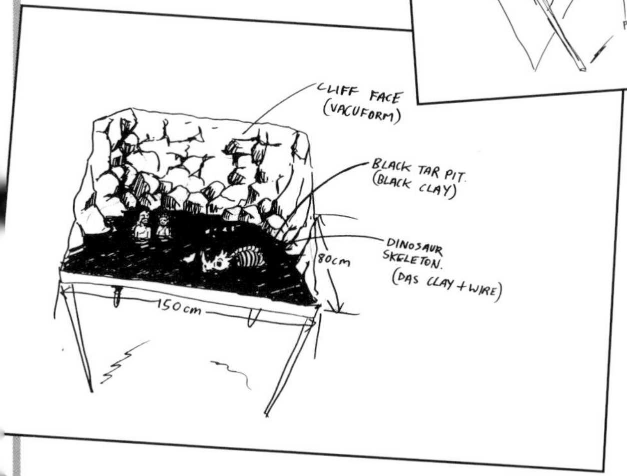

▼ This is a partly finished set from the same series shown above.

▲ Screen Play, Barry Purves at Bare Boards. The film used the moving screens typical of a Japanese house to change the scene and carry forward the action without moving the camera or requiring any editing.

MAKING SETS
Making sets for model animation appeals to the toymaker in us. It is a matter of making miniature illusions out of convenient materials.

WATER
Water is an important illusion.
◄ ▲ A sheet of plexiglass is sprayed with color. The unpainted side is the water surface.

◄ ▲ ▼ These pictures show Bev Knowlden working on her film *Backstage with Medusa*. The scale at which she is working can be judged from her hands. All the props and decorations are distorted to carry the magical theme.

WALLS
Creating solid structures from balsa wood, cardboard, or paper. In this case, it is a curved wall from foamboard— a sandwich of foam between two sheets of cardboard.

1 The surface detail and outline are drawn on the cardboard. The shape is then cut out.

2 Because the cardboard is to be shaped in a curve, the back surface is peeled off.

3 Glue supports on with hot glue.

4 The curve of the wall is held in place by tacky putty on the supports.

TREES

Graceful trees and foliage are constantly needed. Although some small-leaf evergreens can be used, real plants are usually either out of scale or will die during shooting.

3 Paint it the desired color.

5 To help support the leaves, glue some copper mesh, sprayed brown, to the branches.

1 Begin with a branch shape of twisted wire.

4 Cut leaves from paper.

6 The leaves can now be attached with hot glue.

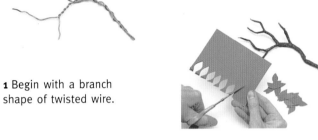

2 Cover it with masking tape for a credible surface.

7 The finished branch is ready to go into place.

SMOKE

The illusion of smoke, as seen here, cannot be achieved with a solid substance.

1 Watercolor is painted on a sheet of glass and animated every other frame to get fluidity.

2 The glass is mounted closer to the camera than the figure, but lined up exactly. The focus will be soft and cloudy.

Filming and Lighting

The first requirement is the stop-frame camera, which must have a pin-registered gate to ensure steady action from frame to frame.

There are various 35mm cameras available – all motor driven. In the 16mm range, Bolex is the most commonly used. Although it is a wind-up camera, it can be adapted to take an electric motor.

For video, you would need a broadcast-quality video camera coupled to either a videotape recorder or digital disk recorder. Even if you are shooting on film, it is useful to have a subsidiary video camera mounted with a disk-based digital recorder, so that you can get instant playback of the movement as you film it.

Besides the cameras, you will require a tripod and a "spreader" to give it a stable base. For frame-by-frame movements of the camera up and down, or pivoting from side to side, a geared head is required. This is a mounting to which the camera is fitted, and its movements can be precisely calibrated for stop-frame shooting. The mechanism must be mechanically geared; hydraulic versions do not give the same precision of control. For lateral and tracking movements, rails are often used with the camera riding on a "dolly" on the rails. A low-cost substitute can be made from rollerskate wheels riding on, or suspended from, standard scaffold poles.

In professional studios, computer-operated motion-control rigs for the camera are now common. These are devices capable of carrying the camera through every dimension of movement and, because of the digital control, repeating the movements identically. This makes many complicated special effects possible.

CAMERA TECHNIQUE The use of the camera is not unlike that in live-shot filming. Shots are planned as long-shot general views, mid-shots, and close-ups, as appropriate for the action. The general appearance of each shot will be designed in the storyboard, and the set constructed so that the camera angles and positions can be achieved.

CAMERAS AND TRIPODS
The equipment carrying the camera must be absolutely steady. However, a mobile camera is also desirable, either at its simplest, swinging from side to side or up and down (panning) or traveling forward and back (tracking). This has meant the development of complex equipment.

▼ The film camera is mounted on a heavy-duty tripod which, with the spreader, gives absolute steadiness. The pan-and-tilt head allows limited movement, but changes of viewpoint mean the whole tripod must be moved. The video camera is lighter and requires a less massive tripod.

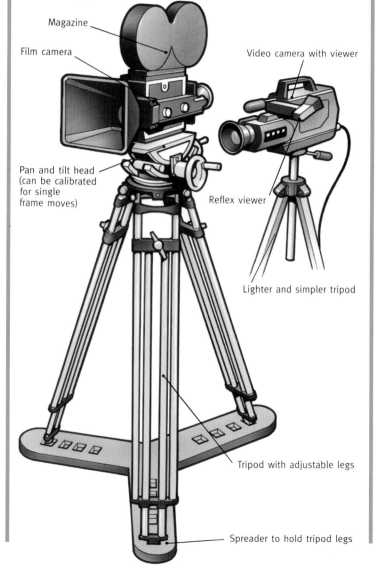

Magazine

Film camera

Video camera with viewer

Pan and tilt head (can be calibrated for single frame moves)

Reflex viewer

Lighter and simpler tripod

Tripod with adjustable legs

Spreader to hold tripod legs

MAKING CAMERAS MOVE

The obstacles to be overcome in devising ways of making the camera mobile are first the set and the objects in it, and second the need not to obstruct the lighting.

▼ This system of suspending the camera from rails allows it to move within a constricting set (say, following something along a corridor) or to pan alongside the set, or a moving object.

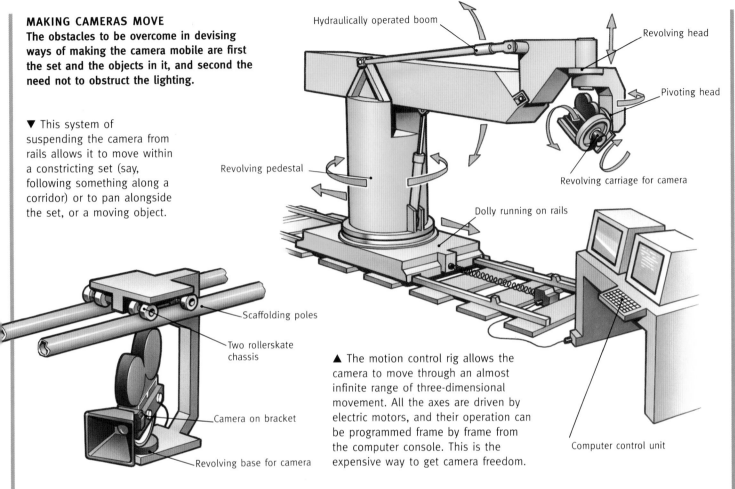

Hydraulically operated boom

Revolving head

Pivoting head

Revolving pedestal

Revolving carriage for camera

Dolly running on rails

Scaffolding poles

Two rollerskate chassis

Camera on bracket

Revolving base for camera

Computer control unit

▲ The motion control rig allows the camera to move through an almost infinite range of three-dimensional movement. All the axes are driven by electric motors, and their operation can be programmed frame by frame from the computer console. This is the expensive way to get camera freedom.

The order in which you shoot will be determined by convenience. Obviously, all the shots required on each set will be done together, regardless of their place in the story, so that the set can be dismantled and the shooting move on to another. Similarly, all shots requiring the same framing or the same lenses will be done together, again often out of sequence. However, it is just as well to make a rough assembly of the shots before dismantling the set, to check whether an additional close-up or cutaway might be necessary to give perfect sense to a sequence. For example, action prescribed as a single shot in the storyboard could require shooting from more than one angle to make clear what is going on.

LIGHTING The standard lighting of 800-watt redheads and big filler lights may require a 30amp supply in order to be properly controlled through dimmers. Smaller lighting kits may be useful, particularly where space is constricted. Sets of small 50-watt

diachromatic halogen cool spots with built-in reflectors are available. They run on 12-volt current, so they have to be connected through a transformer and are usually wired with a dimmer control for each light.

Lighting is the most important contributor to the mood of a scene. Bright diffused lighting over a whole scene contrasts strongly with one where the lighting is narrowly directed in an otherwise murky set-up. By using colored filters over the lights, you can accentuate the warmth of light in some areas, and the coolness of shadows in others. Complete atmospheres, such as moonlight or the effect of being underwater, are also a matter of controlling the overall color of the lighting.

There is a difference to note when you are lighting for video rather than for film. Video, because of its narrower response, needs a lower contrast in lighting. For film, the bright areas can be brighter and the shadows deeper and richer.

▲ The scene is a general view of an interior lit by late afternoon sun filtered through the slats of a venetian blind.

The main sources of light are **1**, the two 500w fresnel (focusable) lights outside the set pointing at a low angle through the slits of the blinds. Additional fill-in lighting is provided by **2**, a bounced light from a floodlight onto the flat outside the open door and **3**, a similar bounced light to the right of the camera.

LIGHTING THE SET AND THE CHARACTERS

Lighting can be used to direct the audience's understanding of your film and is an integral part of the action. In controlling the lighting, remember that an audience will grasp what is merely implied, so do not overstate things.

Will the film be served by a high-key look (with low contrast, as for comedy) or low key (high contrast as in *film noir*)? What quality do you want, soft or hard? What coloring?

Work out the main lighting positions and the direction of the lamps. Use filters and screens to color them until the main sculptural effects are complete. Try to keep a good separation between objects in the foreground and the background. This helps composition and will give more flexibility in maintaining the lighting continuity from shot to shot. If you have to move a light for a reverse shot or a different angle, the audience can be confused by a different lighting of the same object.

▶ Some lights have lenses so that their beams can be diffused or focused. Others have a simple flooding effect. There are various ways of cutting off the light to places where it is not wanted by shutters (called barn doors), "flags" which are screens mounted on stands, or "cukes," screens with cut shapes to throw mottled shadows.

800w "redhead"

300w "junior"

100w spot or flood

Flood lamp

Mini light

Snoot

Scrum filters, total and partial

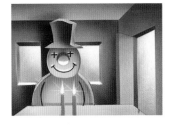

▲ This is lighting for a seated figure in close-up. Moonlight comes through the window behind him, and his face is candle-lit.

Here the two 500w lights, **1**, are given a blue filter, and the beam is diffused for the moonlight effect. Overhead, **2**, a soft orange-tone light is directed downward to reinforce the candle effect. An orange glow is bounced through the doorway, **3**. **4** is a reflector to bounce back some of the blue moonlight. The candles, **5**, are small projector bulbs wired to a dimmer.

▲ Again, a close-up of the interior lit for a sunny day at midday. The light comes from one direction lighting the foreground figure against a shadowy background.

The main lighting is as for the first set, but with the 500w lights, **1**, placed higher and with the beams diffused and interrupted by a screen of "cukes," i.e., a card with holes cut into it to simulate foliage breaking up the light, **2**.

▲ A romantic lamp-lit two-shot of a couple on either side of the table. The principal light coming from an overhead source at low level, and with a warm shadowy background.

The Tiffany lamp, **1**, providing the overhead source, is lit with a projector bulb. From each side 300w (pepper) lamps, **2**, with diffusers and "flags" to limit the spread of the light, illuminate each character. A gold reflector, **3**, is used to bounce a fill-in light into the shadows.

Soundtracks

It could be argued that the quality of the sound with an animated film is more important than that of the picture. A good robust or effectively sensitive sound track can often support humdrum animation, while impressive images are weakened by poor sound.

Sound is a very important consideration. The rhythm and pattern of music can give a solid timing base to someone with a limited experience of composing in a time-based medium. And, as everyone knows, music is vital in creating a mood.

For character animation, the choice and direction of the voicing is just as important in fleshing out the personality of the characters as their drawing. When UPA, in the 1950's, initiated a revolt against the naturalism of the Disney style, they strengthened the appeal of their formalized characters by giving them rich and bizarre voices and dialogue. Unfortunately, this development resulted in the weak material of television series which began to rely on nonstop dialogue scripts accompanied by uninventive pictures.

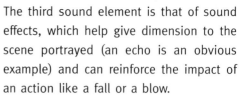

The third sound element is that of sound effects, which help give dimension to the scene portrayed (an echo is an obvious example) and can reinforce the impact of an action like a fall or a blow.

In this chapter we will try to deal with the choice and preparation of the sound elements and how they are physically organized to relate to the picture.

Sound and Music

The three usual elements of a sound track—voice, music, and sound effects—all have the power to appeal to the imagination; brought together, they can do more than half the work of the film.

Sometimes films are made to existing music, pop videos being an example. These projects are nearly always the result of a commission by a recording company. Generally, to use a favorite piece of music as the basis for a film will involve you in heavy payments to the holders of rights. Not only composers, but performers and recording companies as well, demand payment which may run into thousands of dollars.

COMMISSIONING AND RECORDING If you are going to commission music for a piece of animation, it is important that the musician should be involved at the storyboard stage. Clear guidance can be given, based on stop-watch timings of the sequences from the storyboard. Printed forms called bar-sheets give you a framework in which you can lay out in terms of seconds and minutes the proposed action and your notion of the length and mood of the music. If the music is planned in sections, you can adjust any difference between the planned timings and the final cut length by either spacing the sections out or overlapping them on a sound dissolve. If songs are recorded for the film, it is useful to keep the voice and the backing track separate. This gives you flexibility at the final mixing stage and will be a necessity if at a later date you make a version in another language.

When you approach a musician, bear in mind that you will be using only part of his/her skill. You are seeking merely a contributory element to your film, whereas their training and inclination is to make something complete in itself. You will rarely need the full luscious flood of orchestral music continuing for minutes at a time; animation requires a spare, open approach—chamber music or a small jazz combo, perhaps.

The development of multi-track tape, synthesizers, and sampling techniques have now

Further Information
☞
Timing and synchronization, p.102

FILMS DESIGNED TO MUSIC The most celebrated example of a film inspired by music is Disney's *Fantasia*. Other film makers such as Len Lye and Norman McLaren have related picture and music closely.

▼ ▲ These are frames from Bruno Bozzetto's parody of *Fantasia*, *"Allegro non troppa."* He directed sequences sometimes by other animators, which were inspired by well-known pieces of classical music.

made it possible for musicians to supply complete tracks, even with the sound effects incorporated by the composer. The final recording is usually left until the picture has been finally edited. A composer will work to a video transfer of your cutting copy. This has a visual and an audio time code which corresponds to a similar time code in the composer's own recording equipment so that exact sync can be guaranteed.

LIBRARY MUSIC There are many companies that keep libraries of ready-made background music composed and recorded in convenient sections for editing and combining. Sometimes this music can be very apt, but it is a bit like making a cake from a mix instead of using your own ingredients. Normally a fee must be paid to a recording copyright organization for the use of such music, but the cost is much less than acquiring the rights to commercially recorded music, either pop or classical.

VOICE Dialogue, particularly if there are to be animated mouth movements, is recorded at the beginning of production. Choose voices for your characters in the same way as you design their appearance, aiming for contrasts that emphasize individual personalities. The voice should add another dimension to the character, and only secondarily should it be regarded as a vehicle for the words. Pitch—high or low, methods of speech, clarity of enunciation, and dialect are all matters to consider.

It is possible to make "actuality" recordings of people's speech in everyday situations and use them as a basis for animation. This method is most successful where the voice is not given to a human character, but is distanced in some way, by being given to an animal or even an object which represents the speaker.

SOUND EFFECTS Almost the first principle of sound effects, particularly for animation, is that there is no connection between the object in the picture and the origin of the sound. Horses do not make the well-known clip-clop noise; half a coconut shell does.

Standard libraries of sound effects used as they come are more or less useless for animation because the action of animation is too compact. A real car takes an age to go into the distance compared with the animation of the same action. A noise from a library disk or tape may be a good starting point for the sound you want, but it will need speeding up or slowing down, distorting or playing backward before it sounds right and is the right length.

Time spent in a recording studio making your own noises can be expensive, but the cost has to be weighed against the tedium of reviewing hours of library sound effects, of which most will be totally unsuitable and a few only second best. A solution is to make your own effects in a room of your own, provided it can be reasonably free of ambient noise. Using a DAT recorder, you can

MAKING SOUND EFFECTS
Creating the sound you can hear in your head using ordinary domestic objects can be a very frustrating pursuit. It can also be fun.

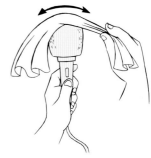

Surge of the sea by dragging cloth

Swanee whistle for "falling".

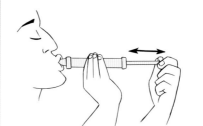

Crumpling paper for fire

Wild animals by distorting pet sounds

Rudimentary echo chamber (metal trashcan)

Coconuts or hollow boxes for hooves

Tapping pencils for heels

Ripping cloth for zipper

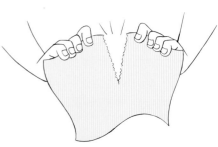

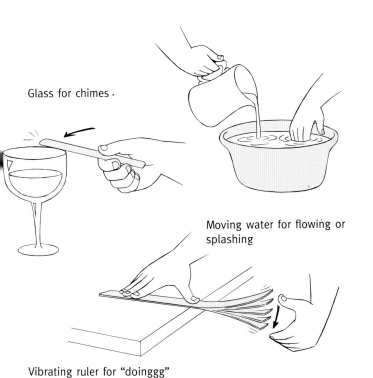

Glass for chimes.

Moving water for flowing or splashing

Vibrating ruler for "doinggg"

put together a collection of the sounds you want, and if they need further treatment, you can have that done when you transfer them to the magnetic film or videotape you will prepare and edit your sound on.

In some ways, analog quarter-inch tape is the ideal medium for recording sound effects for animation. It can be physically cut to assemble the best selection of sounds before transfer, which saves on stock. Also, quarter-inch tape recorders frequently have more than one speed so that sounds recorded at one speed can be played back, for transfer, at another to get a character for the sound you want. The perfect quarter-inch machine has progressively variable recording speeds, but they are not common. A synthesizer, besides being useful for music, can be a good source for sound effects. Try to record all your sound effects at a middle level. Then they can be made louder or softer at the final sound mixing. If they are too loud or too soft, there may be problems in raising or lowering the volume at the mixing stage. Finally, don't forget that you will need some form of atmosphere—even if it is only an open mike in a silent room (known as "buzz track"). Otherwise, your voice and effects will seem to cut in and out of very dead silence.

MUSIC BRIEFING
This is a sample of a chart to brief a composer to prepare music ahead of production so that you can animate precisely to it.

The action timings are an estimate from the storyboard; the dialogue has probably already been recorded, so you have absolute lengths for it. By getting the music composed in separate sections, you can adjust the lengths against the dialogue for a final version.

Timing and Synchronization

If you require exact sync for either voice or music, you will need to do some sort of frame-by-frame analysis before planning the animation.

This analysis is written on a bar-sheet for the music, and directly on the animation dope sheet for the voice, if you intend lip sync.

VOICE To analyze voice sync, it is best to have the voice recording on film (either 16mm or 35mm) which can be turned by hand through a synchronizer, and the beginnings and ends of the sounds which make up the speech marked on the film. Then using either a roll of film with numbered frames on it, or the footage and frame counter on the synchronizer, you can work out how many frames are taken up with each sound. Don't forget that what you are marking is purely the sound—forget the spelling of the words. For example, "The quick brown fox" spoken by a Southerner will analyze as THUH KWIHK BRAHN FAWK. The phonetic letters are the author's own choice. Anyone can make up a phonetic alphabet, provided it accurately represents the sounds without reference to written spelling. It is important to distinguish between the different vowel sounds which are normally written with the same letters: o as in sore; OH as in bone; AW as in hot, and so on. As you can see from the example, some sounds may last only one frame. If your character is moving on twos, it is an unnecessary refinement to give a separate mouth movement for each frame (and there may not be a spare cel level), and so you have to compromise and assign the sounds two frames at a time.

MUSIC The beginnings and ends of musical phrases can be discovered by hand-turning on a synchronizer, as with the voice. But hand-turning of music produces a sound too slurred for most purposes. Marking beats must be done at a constant running speed on a motor-driven synchronizer or on an editing machine. Run the section you are working on two or three times, beating time on

Further Information
☞
Sound and music, p.99

MOUTH MOVEMENT FOR LIP SYNC

The way in which you deal with lip sync will vary. If the style of annotation is bold and the voice character is exaggerated, the mouth movement can be very positive. If the voice is less defined and the character drawing more naturalistic, mouth movement will be more restrained. The dope sheet gives important information regarding lip sync.

TH (with tongue)

R and N (indeterminate consonant)

K

AH

OO = W

F (teeth over lips)

I (with teeth)

O (short o)

B (compressed teeth)

S (often several frames)

DUCTION | SEQUENCE | SCENE 11/12 'MR LEMMING'

The dope sheet with columns: ACTION | DIAL | EXTRA | 8 | 7 | 6 | 5 | 4 | 3 | 2 | 1 | EXTRA | CAMERA INSTRUCTIONS

Frame markings (EXTRA column): M7 (1), M2 (5), M3 (6), M4 (9), M5 (11), M3 (13), M6 (15), M7 (17), M8 (19), I (23), M7 (24), M9 (26), M10 (28), M3 (30), M11 (32), M7 (38)

Text on action column: THUH, KW, LH, KB, R, FAW, X

MCB 3

(Bar chart showing frame timings from 0 to 376, with second markings: 1 SEC 24, 2 SEC 48, 3 SEC 72, 5 SEC 120, 6 SEC 144, 7 SEC 168, 9 SEC 216, 10 SEC 240, 11 SEC 266, 13 SEC 312, 14 SEC 336, 15 SEC 360)

DRUM BEATS, START INSTRUMENTAL, GLISS.

* BEATS ~~~ FLUTE ~~~ HARP

BAR CHART

Music is marked up on a bar chart like this in numbers of frames.

▶ The editor has probably been told what information the animator needs to know and works accordingly. Usually, the beats of the rhythm and specific instrumental passages are singled out. To mark the progress of every instrument would be too complicated.

◀▲ These heads give some idea of the principle behind mouth movements. Es and Ss tend to show teeth. TH is normally expressed with a protruding tongue. V and F require the teeth to come over the lower lip. Other consonants such as L, R, N, D and T are neutral in character. Vowels need the mouth open to a greater or lesser extent. OO, which is also the shape for W, requires the lips to gather into a sort of tube. The dope sheet (above) shows the number of frames for each mouth movement (left).

the film with a wax pencil leaving a clear mark. Make an average of your marks from the three runs and firm up the marking. Then run the music again, watching your marks go over the sound head, while listening to check that they are accurate.

It is possible, though not so easy, to do this sort of sound analysis from a videotape, but you need a video editing machine with a seconds and frames counter. By using the search control, you can listen for the sound points you want, but it is a less positive method than with film because it is not so easy to identify the frame exactly.

FILM AND VIDEO SPEEDS There is a synchronization problem you need to be aware of, particularly related to music. The running speed of projected film in cinemas is 24 frames a second. For video and TV, it is 25. Thus, 4,500 frames or three minutes of video runs 7½ seconds longer when projected as film (3 minutes at 24 frames a second = 4,320 frames). If you make a film to last 3 minutes at 24 frames a second and transfer it to video for the musician to compose to, he will be working to a time length of 2 minutes 52 seconds and 20 frames. In transferring his music from digital disk tape onto film, it is important that the recording of the transfer is made at 25 frames per second to restore the right number of frames for 24-frame projection, i.e. 172.8 seconds x 25 = 4,320.

Themes

The pictures featured in the following pages are merely static representatives of what are essentially moving images. Bear in mind that even if two successive film frames are presented, that is only one-twelfth of a second. It is the film as a whole which is significant, not isolated images—these can give a false impression of the whole. The categories they are in, therefore, refer not to the techniques or the nature of each image, but to the intention of the filmmakers in each case.

Animation has now proved itself capable of many moods and varied depths of feeling. This selection of pictures will, hopefully, convey that variety.

These frames of Jerry in action from the classic series of MGM's *Tom and Jerry* shorts can serve as a symbol for cartoon films as a whole. Always comic, no one would claim for them a depth of dramatic feeling, although they were often successful in conveying pathos.

Dramatic

The use of animation to give dramatic strength to a story is the quality looked for in assigning works to this category. It is only in the last 20 years that animators have developed visual language which gives them the confidence to attempt non-comic material.

▼ *Achilles,* Barry Purves, Bare Boards Productions. In contrast to *Rigoletto* (right), Barry Purves' marvelously real puppets act out a drama without being confined to an imitative format. Character and drama are conceived together.

◀ *Rigoletto*, Barry Purves, Bare Boards Productions. This illustration comes from a half-hour version of the opera. The puppets and decor are astonishingly beautiful, while the animation is flawless. One wonders, however, whether so perfect an animation, in a truncated form, of a live performance of the opera is a necessary endeavor.

▶ *Animal Farm*, Halas and Batchelor. This is one of the earliest feature-length cartoon films with a serious dramatic intention. It was certainly the first in Britain. Although the main part of the action is with animal characters, the overall design retained a more or less natural appearance for animals and humans. Their hands have four fingers!

◀ Caroline Leaf's *The Street*, for the National Film Board of Canada. This earns its place in the dramatic category because of the success with which the Mordecai Richler story is translated into appropriate images and movement. The technique used is paint on glass.

◀ *The Nightmare Before Christmas*, Tim Burton, Skellington Productions, directed by Henry Selick. Alternating with ease between live-shot features and animation, Tim Burton has a sure grip on narrative which he uses to convey dark thoughts about us all.

▼ *The House of Flame*, Kihachito Kawamoto. Superb naturalistic puppets performing a story as dramatic as any of the works of Kurosawa.

▲ *The Simpsons*, Klasky-Csupo Productions. These films, based on comic strip characters created by Matt Groening, are included because of the maturity and intelligence of their storylines. Although the characters are broad caricatures, the tenor of their lives is familiar to everyone.

▶ *Yellow Submarine*, George Dunning. This picture, like all the others on these two pages, comes from films of mixed images. George Dunning set about matching the Beatles music with the visual imagination of his collaborators Heinz Edelmann, Charlie Jenkins, and Bill Sewell. A "quest" narrative held the fireworks together.

◀*Taxandria*, Raoul Servais. Although a skilled and distinguished animator, Servais has found satisfaction most often in this dramatic combination of live and drawn work. Perhaps it is explained by his connection with Magritte and the Surrealists.

▼ *The Secret Adventures of Tom Thumb*, Dave Borthwick, Bolex Brothers. It is a natural approach to a tale of midgets and giants to mix the media in which they appear. Puppets and human actors were often filmed together.

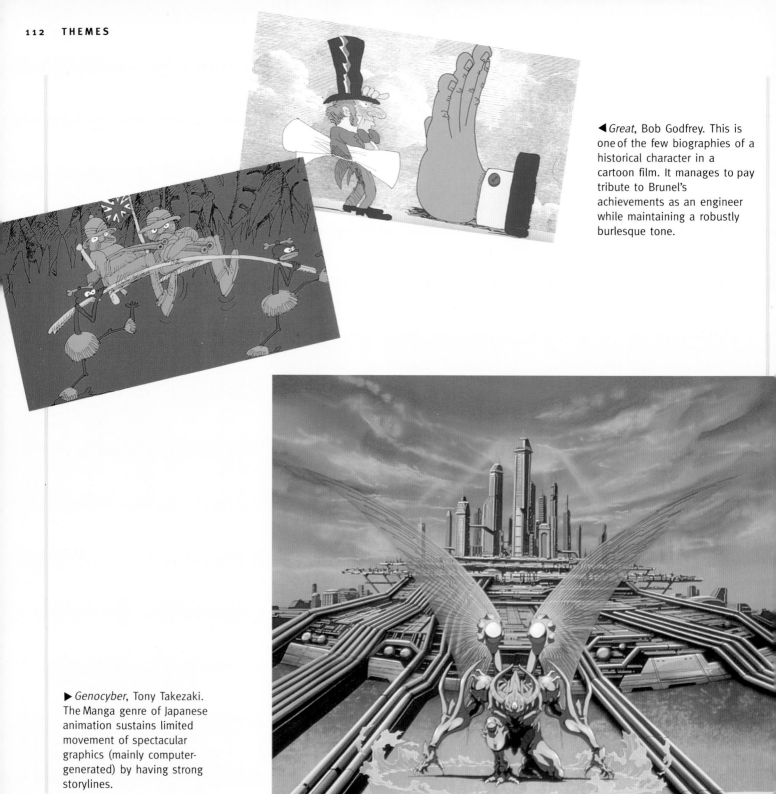

◄ *Great*, Bob Godfrey. This is one of the few biographies of a historical character in a cartoon film. It manages to pay tribute to Brunel's achievements as an engineer while maintaining a robustly burlesque tone.

► *Genocyber*, Tony Takezaki. The Manga genre of Japanese animation sustains limited movement of spectacular graphics (mainly computer-generated) by having strong storylines.

◀ *Screen Play*, Barry Purves, Bare Boards Productions. Purves used the conventions of Japanese drama to tell a terrifying story. The puppets and the scenery are manipulated in a way which is helped by the rigid rules. It lasts ten minutes without a single cut.

▼*Nasruddin* (also known as *The Thief*), Richard Williams. This still is taken from the design stage of Williams' feature—the culmination of years of struggle. It contains spectacular sequences from a master of full animation.

◀ *Alice*, Jan Švankmajer. This master of animated objects has always blithely disregarded the frontier between the real and the imagined, which makes Lewis Carroll's Alice a natural choice for him. The film is in color.

▶ *Death and the Mother*, Ruth Lingford for Channel 4 (UK). By contrast with Jan Švankmajer's piece, left, this work is deliberately black and white following the conventions of woodcut. Executed by computer, it shows that painterly values are possible by those means. The story is based on a Grimm fable.

▶ *The Conspirators of Pleasure*, Jan Švankmajer. Further evidence of this filmmaker's blending of more than one convention of picture-making.

Lyrical

The choices for this category have been guided by selecting those films where the intention has not been to tell a connected narrative. These films are notable for the impression they produce, partly from the high quality of the image, but mostly for the poetic force given to the images by the concept driving the film.

The Mill, Petra Freeman for Channel 4 Television (UK). The images are drawn from memories of childhood in this good example of painting on glass.

Flying Circus, Maureen Selwood. It is no coincidence that this film is also based on memories of childhood, a common wellspring for films of this kind. The use of varied techniques throughout the film allows for changes of mood.

◄ *Lakme*, Pascal Roulin, from the Opera Imaginaire series, Pascavision. This is one of a series of films made by different directors to accompany excerpts from operas. Computer animation in this case produced dream-like transformations and scenes of lyrical beauty.

▲ *Perpetuo*, Josko Marusic, Zagreb Film. The Zagreb studio was one of the first to take advantage of the artistic liberation which affected animation in the 1950s and 1960s. This work is that of a painter and designer who found a new métier in animation.

◀ *Entropy II*, Woojin Chang. An example of the ease with which digital methods can create splendid effects as well as mixing of media and figure animation. Such blending of image is likely to become more and more common as audiences become accustomed to such uses of technology.

▼ ▶ *My Favorite Things That I Love*, Janet Perlman. This film is another example of the personal reverie. The upper picture is from a sequence using photo cut-outs as well as cel animation. The lower picture is made up of black paper cut-outs coloured with pastel.

▶ *Paralysis*, Motoko and Takashi Tokuyama. This film is the work of a husband and wife partnership who create installations for exhibitions as well as puppet animated films.

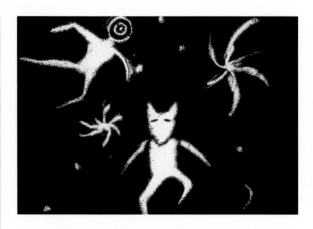

◄ *The Dancing Bulrushes*, Joanna Priestley. This is a sprightly sand animation. The moving figures and shapes are created by clearing patches in the sand over a light, with the ground remaining dark.

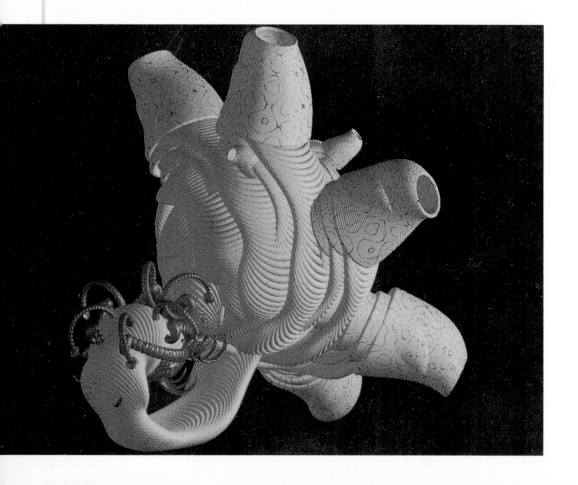

◄ *Tuskio, Organic Television*, William Latham. This work by one of the earliest experimenters with purely abstract computer animation shows the complexity of moving three-dimensional shape that is now possible using purely mathematical concepts.

◄ *Crofton Road SE5*, Gerd Gockell at Anigraf. The images of this film are a typical example of mixed media, with photographs, painting, and deliberately dislocated collage.

▲ *The Owl Who Married a Goose*, Caroline Leaf and Co Hoedeman for the National Film Board of Canada. In this remarkable film, the technique of sand animation (here with the blacks and whites reversed) was used to reproduce the appearance of Eskimo prints. The story is a traditional Inuit one, and the sound was provided by an Inuit storyteller.

► *Spotless Dominoes*, Philip Hunt. This film was made while Hunt was a student. What it lacks in clarity of communication is made up for by the vivacity of the puppets and the animation, as well as by the impressive mood created by the overall design. The puppets were made of latex built onto a wire armature.

◄ *Corridor of Clowns*, Paul Smith, Raytech (BBS). The work and the mathematical calculation which would have been needed to achieve this moving image by hand is unthinkable. This is virtual reality in action.

▼ *Space and Motion*, Deborah Shachar. By contrast, this is the human hand at its smudgiest. Very broad charcoal drawing, but the action carries a punch.

◄ This drawing from *The Fool Cries for the Evil to Rise*, also by Deborah Shachar, comes from a film in which abstract ideas are worked out by figures not entirely human, but their behavior is close enough to human to give a shudder. The animation is of black drawings on a single level of paper. The sound is as unearthly as the pictures.

Didactic

These are works which aim to carry a message. The humor, design, animation, and story are all contributors to that end. It is a category which can overlap with commissioned work, but it is also one in which we find works which express something personally important to the filmmaker.

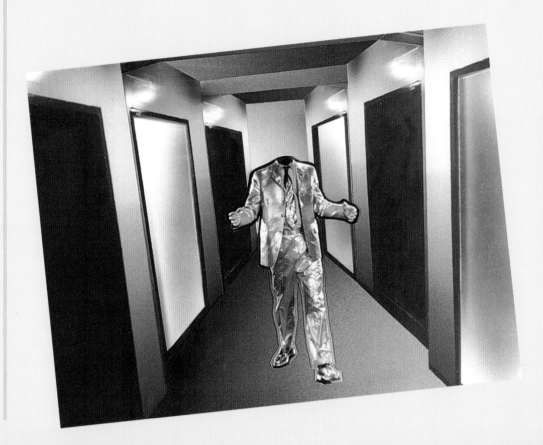

◄ *Headless* by Paul Vester, Speedy Films. A TV commercial for Copperhead cider demonstrating a lively adventurousness of technique, employing animated cutouts and photographic backgrounds.

Every Child, written by Derek Lamb, designed and animated by Eugene Fedorenko for UNICEF, The National Film Board of Canada. These enchanting images are executed on frosted cel. The original artwork is delicately drawn on a field of 4 × 5 inches. The National Film Board has, of course, an honorable tradition in public service films.

▶ A series of cels from *Karate Kids* written and designed by Derek Lamb with additional design and animation by Kai Pindal and Borg Ring. This is another production via The National Film Board of Canada for a United Nations organization, in this case the World Health Organization. It is traditional cel animation, but here the line drawing has been photocopied onto the cel, preserving the animator's original line.

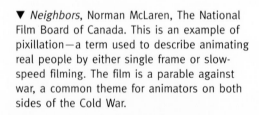

▶ *Neighbors*, Norman McLaren, The National Film Board of Canada. This is an example of pixillation—a term used to describe animating real people by either single frame or slow-speed filming. The film is a parable against war, a common theme for animators on both sides of the Cold War.

▲ *Why me?*, Janet Perlman and Derek Lamb, the National Film Board of Canada. The message in this case was to those confronted with the diagnosis of a terminal illness. As with *Every Child,* the artwork is on a small scale (a 4-inch field this time).

◀ *Hurry-Hurry!* Stefanie Dinkelbach. This again is a film which springs from personal conviction. Dinkelbach's intention is to portray the damage done by adults who fail to understand the importance of time in relation to their children. She used both ordinary puppets and cutouts made from her children's drawings.

▲ *Give Us a Smile*, Leeds Animation Workshop. A film about violence against women. This group makes no attempt to conceal its partisan views in the films it makes. The films are meant to put across a message and employ simple means to do so.

▼ *The Last Air Raid*, *Kumagaya*, Renzo Kinoshita. The animator has a worthy record of satirical attacks on contemporary wickedness. His simple techniques make his meaning direct.

▲ *Some Protection*, Marjut Rimminen. In the sense that this film is based on the experiences of a real individual, it is a documentary. This is, however, a drawn documentary which uses conventional animation to dramatize how those who begin as merely unfortunate may end up defined as criminal.

◀ *The Web*, Lucinda Clutterbuck, Eco Films. This film comes from a series about threatened species. The technique employed varies, but there is substantial use of cut-paper animation to celebrate the rich textures of the animals described.

▼ *Cage of Flame*, Kayla Parker. Although her chosen method is oblique suggestion rather than open preaching, this film conveys the maker's passionate feelings about the physical nature of women. She is an expert in drawing directly on film, but this is normal cel or paper animation.

Commercials

Included here is not only animation commissioned for advertising, but also for other purposes, like title sequences where there is a specific brief for content and length. This is work which sustains many studios and individual animators because it is a field where budgets are often ample so there are opportunities for experimenting with new techniques.

Smart-i-llusions. A British candy commercial (for Smarties). Richard Purdum Productions. Directed by Richard Purdum and Michael Dudok de Wit, designed by Andrzej Dudzinski. This is from a studio renowned for the skill and fluency of its drawn animation, which is allied here to computer imaging.

Mystery, Derek Lamb. Designer
Edward Gorey. This is from a
title sequence for a series of
television programs. The
director has relied on Gorey's
bizarre black-and-white
illustrations to supply the
atmosphere.

▲ A commercial for Levi's 501 jeans, Aaargh! Animation. No effort has been spared here to reach the ultimate in robust vulgarity in a modeled clay pastiche of Hollywood heroism.

▼ Martell's *Legend,* a commercial by Pat Gavin at Hibbert Ralph. Elegantly rendered drawings with some computer assistance in the dimensional drawing, with the whole thing put together by video editing. This quality of rendering can only be feasible at commercial length and with a commercial's budget.

▼ Listerine *Arrows* commercial by Pixar, directed by Jan Pinkava. A demonstration of how digital technology brings together disparate images and blends them into a more or less convincing whole. It is much more convincing in movement than as a still.

▶ MTV logo by Run Wrake. This television station keeps many animators busy creating short station "idents."

▼ *Reputations*, Television program title by Philip Hunt for Pizazz Pictures. These sequences are often, like the commercials, more inventive than the programs they introduce.

▲ *Big and orange*, a commercial for Coca-Cola Fanta by the Bolex Brothers studio. This wonderful machinery was all built for just a few seconds of action.

▶ *Desmond the Dog*, a commercial for NRG Lucozade, designed by Jeff Bastedo from Lost in Space. It is refreshing to see computers used to be funny rather than emptily impressive.

▲ *It's hip to be a square,* for Children's Television Workshop, producers of "Sesame Street," by Candy Kugel for Buzzco Associates. CTW have used puppets and animation to do more good in the world than perhaps any other producer. This is cel animation on still photographs.

▶ These historic frames are from Len Lye's *Colour Box*, 1936. The pattern is drawn or printed by hand directly onto the film stock. The British Post Office allowed the film unit wide liberty in making its publicity films. The tradition, begun with Lye and John Grierson, was followed in the establishment of the National Film Board of Canada, where Norman McLaren, an earlier associate of Lye, achieved preeminence.

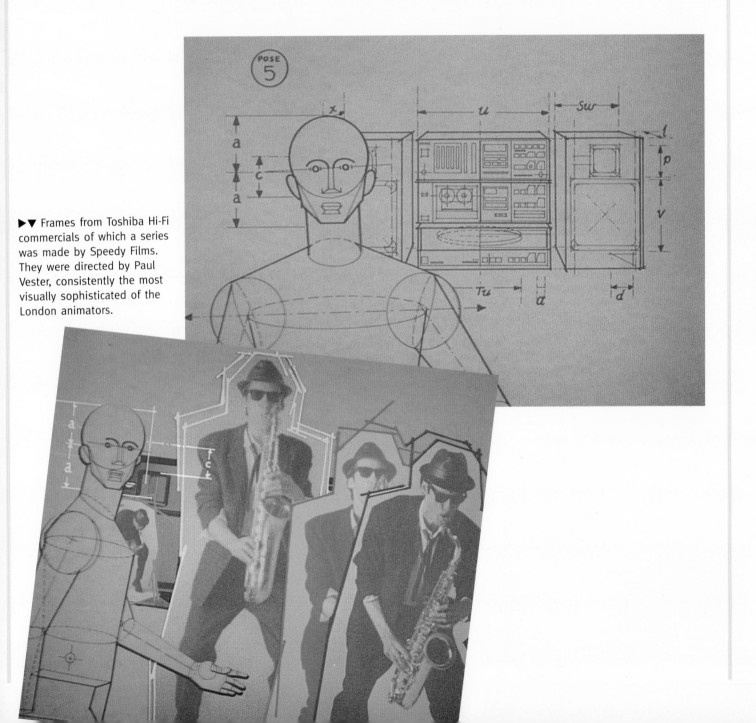

▶▼ Frames from Toshiba Hi-Fi commercials of which a series was made by Speedy Films. They were directed by Paul Vester, consistently the most visually sophisticated of the London animators.

▶ From the Monster Munch campaign by Ken Lidster at Loose Moose. It is curious how, as computer imaging has advanced, the design of traditionally constructed puppet characters has converged with computer styles.

▼ Aquafresh commercial, Pizazz Pictures. Delicately rendered animation with some help from a computer. The restraint of the tones and the softness of textures are pleasing.

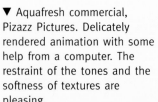

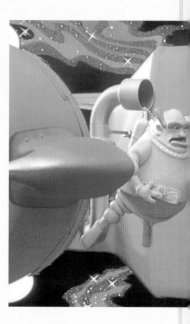

▲ Taste Invaders, Ken Lidster. An even more marked correspondence between traditional models and computer designs, perhaps related to the space theme.

◀ ▲ Angel Delight commercial from the Richard Williams studio. The animators were called on to work with characters of long-standing design not originally intended for animation. The sort of human interaction needed is at odds with the design, but the animators have done their best. Both the background detail and the drawing are excellent. The line is the animator's original line either drawn directly on cel or photocopied.

▶ The commercials shown on these two pages originated from Richard Purdum Productions and are an indication of the versatility of techniques needed for advertising. *Smart-i-llusions* for Nestle, Michael Dudok de Wit and Richard Purdum together. Use of computer techniques combined with traditional drawn work.

▼ *Pop Tarts* by Michael Dudok de Wit combined lively traditional drum work with a computer-generated environment.

▶ *Grasshopper and the Ants* for Merrill Lynch, Richard Purdum. This is a thorough-going example of a "picture book" style carried through in movement. Such work requires a lot of time and great skill at every level of production.

◀ *Rhinestones* for Rotary, animated and directed by Richard Purdum. Again, this is animation based on an established illustration style, although more formalized than *Grasshopper*. The designer is Georgine Strathy.

▼ *The Fox and the Grapes* for Merrill Lynch, Richard Purdum. Traditional drawing for a traditional tale. The treatment of the character animation is well matched to the background.

Children's

To some, it may seem odd to have a separate section of animation for child audiences, since the greatest volume of animation as a whole seems directed at them. Much of this kind of work is produced in bulk to feed television, and it is not particularly interesting from the point of view of technique. We have selected a small representation of the whole.

▼ *The Frog King*, Marjut Rimminen, Smoothcloud Productions. Cel animation on pen and wash backgrounds, from a filmmaker better known for more disturbing subjects.

◄ *When I Grow Up I Want to be a Tiger*, An Vrombaut. An example of a well-designed and animated single short film for children.

◄▲ *Charlie Says,* Richard Taylor. This is from a series made particularly for children under five. Like *Sesame Street*, the entertainment also carried a message. The technique was cutout, but a considerable amount of lip synchronization was attempted.

◄ *A little journey*, Renzo Kinoshita. This is a single 12-minute film using both cel and cutout animation. The general treatment is reminiscent of John Hubley's *Windy Day*. Like a lot of material for children, there is an accompanying ecological message.

◄*Munk and Lemmy—Let's Fly*, AnimaCijas Brigade, Latvia. This represents the other international product familiar to children throughout the world.

▶*Thumbelina*, Lotte Reiniger. Working almost alone, Lotte Reiniger developed in Europe this painstaking style of paper cutout silhouette work for children's entertainment. She had few imitators. Disney was meanwhile developing the noisier, more colorful style which could be mass produced.

▼ *Les Trois Inventeurs*, Michel Ocelot, Production aaa. Exquisite cut-paper work which has used the relief of embossed paper. The method suits the lighthearted view of human inventions and the period in which it is set.

▲ ▶*La Princesse Insensible*, Michel Ocelot, Production aaa. For this children's series, cut-outs and cel animation have been combined. As with his other work, the design is both elegant and charming. The use of elaborate architectural motifs recalls the fairy tales of Perrault and La Fontaine.

▶ *La Reine Cruelle*, from the Cine Si series, Michel Ocelot, produced by La Fabrique. Here Michel Ocelot follows the tradition of Lotte Reiniger in using cut paper for silhouette animation, but he adds to it rich coloring.

All the pictures on these two pages are from productions of Storm TV (formerly Filmfair).

▲ *Astrofarm.* The company has also produced puppet work for children's television series. These pleasantly bizarre animals have a tactile appeal.

◀ *The Wombles.* This series was markedly successful in creating a believable community of mythical creatures, but relating them to a real place—Wimbledon Common in London. There was a strong connection both with the merchandising of the characters as toys and with pop music. This is very often the way in which such series are financed.

◀ *White Bear's Secret.* A longer film, based on an established story, extracting the maximum charm from the cozy appeal of bear characters.

▲ ▶ *Treasure Island*, a television series. By converting the characters of *Treasure Island* to animals, the producers achieved two results. First, they have characters more internationally than human ones. Second, they give themselves more liberty to expand the events beyond the original plot—as they need to do for a series.

▶ *Shoe People*. Again, non-human characters are a useful way of getting the widest acceptance of a series. No legs to animate either.

Comic

This category contains those works where the intention of the maker has been primarily to provoke laughter, although more complicated themes and ideas may often be at work behind the laughter.

◀An image from *Sleepy Guy*, an in-house release from Pacific Data Images. The computer has been used successfully to create a comic figure with character rather than the usual gloomy robot.

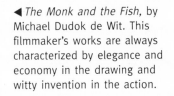 *The Monk and the Fish*, by Michael Dudok de Wit. This filmmaker's works are always characterized by elegance and economy in the drawing and witty invention in the action.

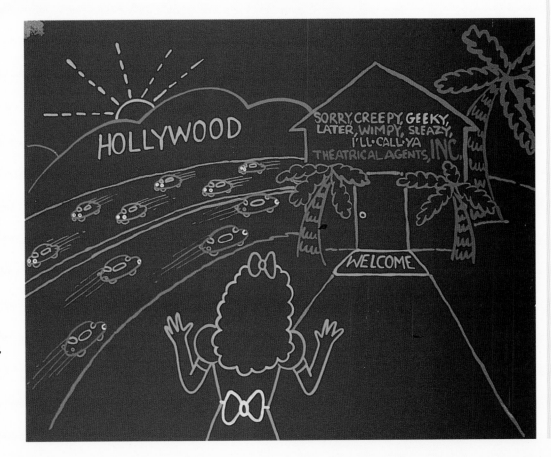

▶ *Snowie and the Seven Dorps*, by Candy Kugel, Buzzco Associates. The bright line on the black background conveys the sinister glitter of Tinseltown which is the film's theme.

◀ *Great*, Bob Godfrey. Although the film from which this came is featured elsewhere as a Dramatic work, it would be unfair to omit Bob Godfrey from the Comic category since it is in that genre that he is strongest.

▲ *Daffy Duck* and *Bugs Bunny*, Warner Brothers. The typical Hollywood cartoon of the 1930's and 1940's from the big studios. Skilled cel animations and full of zip. This image makes a happy link to the slapstick vaudeville tradition which influenced so much of this work. Note the joke "Oscar."

▲▶ *Sing Beast Sing* (above) by Marv Newland at International Rocketship and *Mrs Heart Rate* (right) by Kurtz and Friends. These are an interesting contrast with the Warner Brothers material. Same zip, same skill, same technique of cel animation. But this is 50 years on, the studios are small independents, the graphic styles are freer and the climate of humor more bizarre.

◄ Oh, what bliss! All the joy of full-blooded character creation in *Looney, Looney, Looney Bugs*, a Bugs Bunny short from Warner Brothers. Probably by Chuck Jones.

◄ Every resource of grotesque distortion both in design and animation employed to comic ends. *The Bed Bug* from the "Beastly Behaviour" series by Andy Wyatt of Honeycomb Animation.

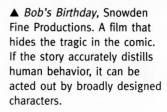

▲ *Bob's Birthday*, Snowden Fine Productions. A film that hides the tragic in the comic. If the story accurately distills human behavior, it can be acted out by broadly designed characters.

◄ The more formalized style of UPA was taken up enthusiastically in Europe. This example from a parody Western by Bruno Bozzetto, entitled *West and Soda*, shows the elegance of Italian graphic design in the backgrounds.

◄ *Gogs*, Michael Mort and Deiniol Morris, Aaargh! Animation. This still is from one of the films in a vigorous series set among dinosaurs and the cave men of prehistory.

The End of the World In Four Seasons, Paul Driessen, working at the National Film Board of Canada. Driessen's gift for finding the most unexpected uses of the film frame is demonstrated here. The color illustration shows how several stories are accommodated simultaneously in the frame. The reproduction of part of his storyboard gives an idea of how he develops such a complex idea.

Bringing it All Together

Making animated films is generally a group activity. Like jazz, it is a field where each individual contribution creates a whole that is greater than the sum of the parts.

In the best studios, everyone competes, not to improve their status or to increase their salary, but to make the most useful contribution to a work that they love. This is the sort of shared spirit that a wise director can inspire and benefit from. The critical point for animators or designers comes when they are no longer exercising only their own skills, but have to call upon the skills of others. The prime aim is to shape the work as you want it, but you must also allow your collaborators and assistants room to use their powers. Think of Duke Ellington.

THE SMALL STUDIO There are many studios in which the regular staff number no more than four or five. Studios of this kind can take on productions of considerable size. As a small group, they have the advantage of a mutual rapport and will also be in contact with skilled and experienced freelance outworkers.

The permanent nucleus of such a unit will probably be headed by an established animator/designer, or perhaps two working in partnership. If they are prudent, they will also have a third partner who functions as a producer, responsible for finding and developing new projects, as well as keeping the finances of the studio properly organized. There might also be one skilled key animator, with the rest of the animation drawing, where necessary, being done by outside animators and assistants. For cel work, where required, there would be someone with a thorough background in trace and paint, probably a former checker in a big studio. He/she would handle the putting out and receiving back of the cel work from outside artists and making sure it is properly organized for camera. The same person, called a produc-

---

Further Information
☞
Cel, p. 52

SYSTEMS OF PRODUCTION

Keeping production mishaps to a minimum depends on clear communication both up and down the team as well as across from the animators to the background department and editors.

▶ There must be very comprehensive and clear model sheets for everyone to follow; and everyone, at all levels in the process, must make sure that unambiguous instructions go with all work that passes from them to the next person down the line. The dope sheet, which shows the sequences of drawings and gives instructions to the cameraman on camera field and moves, is the basic "score" which is the basis of everyone's work from the key animator to the final shooting or recording.

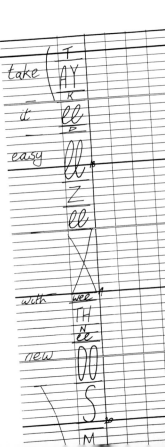

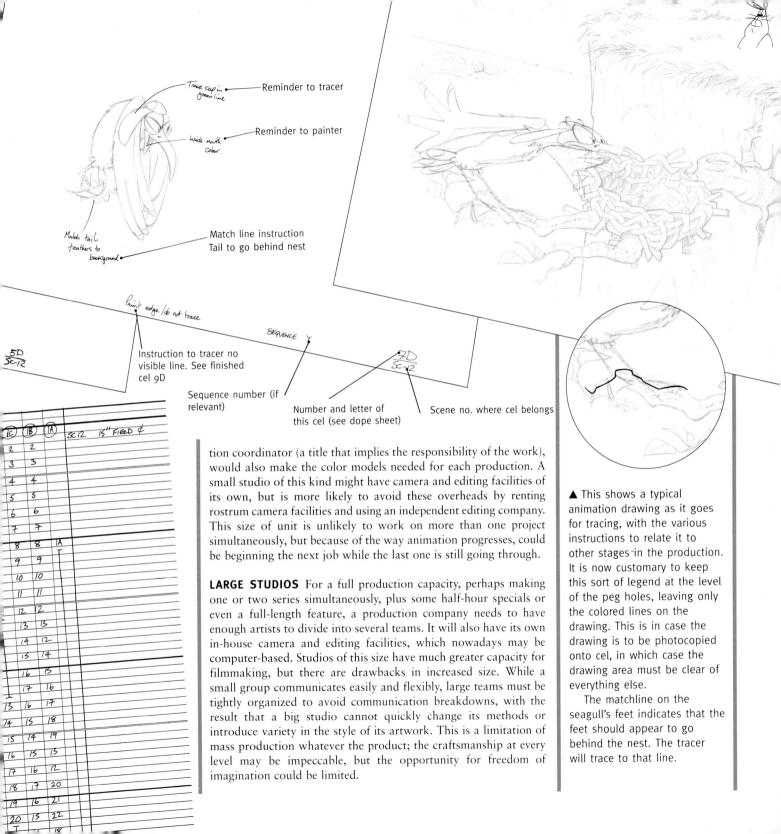

Trace cap in green line — Reminder to tracer

Inside mouth color. — Reminder to painter

Match tail feathers to background —

Match line instruction
Tail to go behind nest

Paint edge / do not trace

SEQUENCE

5D
SC-12

7D
SC-12

Instruction to tracer no
visible line. See finished
cel 9D

Sequence number (if
relevant)

Number and letter of
this cel (see dope sheet)

Scene no. where cel belongs

1C	1B	1A			
			SC 12	15" FIELD ¢	
2	2				
3	3				
4	4				
5	5				
6	6				
7	7				
8	8	1A			
9	9	T			
10	10				
11	11				
12	12				
13	13				
14	12				
15	14				
16	15				
17	16				
13	16	17			
14	15	18			
15	14	19			
16	13	13			
17	16	12			
18	17	20			
19	16	21			
20	15	22			
T		18			

tion coordinator (a title that implies the responsibility of the work), would also make the color models needed for each production. A small studio of this kind might have camera and editing facilities of its own, but is more likely to avoid these overheads by renting rostrum camera facilities and using an independent editing company. This size of unit is unlikely to work on more than one project simultaneously, but because of the way animation progresses, could be beginning the next job while the last one is still going through.

LARGE STUDIOS For a full production capacity, perhaps making one or two series simultaneously, plus some half-hour specials or even a full-length feature, a production company needs to have enough artists to divide into several teams. It will also have its own in-house camera and editing facilities, which nowadays may be computer-based. Studios of this size have much greater capacity for filmmaking, but there are drawbacks in increased size. While a small group communicates easily and flexibly, large teams must be tightly organized to avoid communication breakdowns, with the result that a big studio cannot quickly change its methods or introduce variety in the style of its artwork. This is a limitation of mass production whatever the product; the craftsmanship at every level may be impeccable, but the opportunity for freedom of imagination could be limited.

▲ This shows a typical animation drawing as it goes for tracing, with the various instructions to relate it to other stages in the production. It is now customary to keep this sort of legend at the level of the peg holes, leaving only the colored lines on the drawing. This is in case the drawing is to be photocopied onto cel, in which case the drawing area must be clear of everything else.

The matchline on the seagull's feet indicates that the feet should appear to go behind the nest. The tracer will trace to that line.

Post Production

This term usually means everything that is done between the completion of shooting combined with all the sync sound, and the final form of the film.

The sync sound is usually the dialogue tracks, although some music and effects may have been prerecorded to provide synchronization with parts of the animation. The stages of completion differ, depending on whether all the processes are being done as film editing or as video and electronic editing.

For film, the stages are as follows:
1 Final picture editing including marking up for lab opticals.
2 Laying all remaining sound tracks in sync with this.
3 Sound tracks mixed to a final master (magnetic), either mono or stereo.
4 Picture cutting copy and all negative material to negative cutter.
5 Picture negative in two rolls (A & B) to laboratory with cutting copy for color grading.
6 Laboratory makes first trial print. If necessary, color grading corrected to your satisfaction. Further trial print.
7 At this stage, if the animation is for television, the print will be mute (no sound) and will be transferred to broadcast tape or disk with the sound from the master mix (3).
8 If the film is for theater projection, the magnetic sound will be transferred to an optical negative for making married prints.

EDITING AND MARKING UP If the animation has been sensibly planned, there will be little cutting to do except for joining the scenes together. Once the cutting copy is assembled, however, the whole film should be reviewed for general pace and effectiveness. If further cutting is done, the picture and sync sound should be cut simultaneously to preserve the synchronization. From this stage on, there should be no further alteration to the length.

The finished cutting copy (known as the "work print") must run at the length of the final film. Where one scene is to dissolve into another, the overlap must be cut out and the transition marked on the cutting copy.

> **Further Information**
> ☞
> Sound track, p.98

LAYING SOUNDTRACKS At the start of editing, the

Everything to the right of the synchronizer heads is in sync and should not be touched

Sound heads

Head of film

Sync marks on leaders

Add all new sound and cutting done to left of synchronizer

Small ground glass screen for viewing picture

THE SYNCHRONIZER
Using a machine like this to maintain sync between picture and several sound tracks may seem like steam-age mechanics in an age of electronic pulses, but many people prefer to handle sound in this way.

▲ The main shaft of the synchronizer carries four sprocketed pairs of wheels welded to it. Three are for sound and one for picture.

MARKING OPTICALS
The cutting copy which you edit must run at the same length as the sound. Where opticals are to be introduced, the question of overlap arises.

▼ Second half of the fade out of scene X, and first half of the fade in of scene Y, are cut off, and a join is made where the middle of the dissolve will occur. Cutting copy is marked with diagonal lines.

The cutting copy (print) marked up for a dissolve

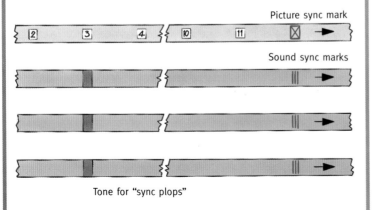

MARKING FOR TRACK LAYING ON A SYNCHRONIZER
The picture mark is put on the Academy leader at the 12-foot mark from the first frame of picture. Level with that, across all the tracks are the three bars of the sound gate mark.

▼ Running the picture and all the tracks together down to the 3-foot mark on the picture leaders, a single frame of tone is then inserted in all the sound tracks.

Tone for "sync plops"

beginning of the picture has an Academy leader joined to it. Any sync sound already laid to the picture also has a leader with a mark which keeps it in parallel with the picture. All other music and effects tracks must be marked in the same way. The sound at this stage will be in the form of sprocketed magnetic film. While the remaining sound tracks are being assembled, they must remain synchronized with the picture throughout. This is done on a picture-synchronizer (also known as a comp editor). Any number of tracks can be assembled, but the synchronizer can usually only handle three at a time. When all the tracks are assembled, the film is now ready for sound mixing—or dubbing.

MIXING THE SOUND As a guide to the dubbing mixer, a chart is prepared giving the placing of every sound on each sound track. The footage, measured from the start of the film, is given for each sound and identified with a name or description. Since the mixer is handling several channels on the mixing desk at once, he or she needs to be sure where each sound is. Sounds which need separate treatment and which follow closely in time should be laid on separate tracks; otherwise, the mixer will not have time to adjust the controls. For example, a soft bang closely followed by a loud one will have to be split onto separate tracks. It is also advisable to keep all effects of the same kind—say footsteps—on one or two tracks together, with no other effects mixed in.

When the final master mix of the sound, either stereo or mono, is finished, it is usual to make another mix without the dialogue. This sound track, known as the "M & E" (music and effects), can be used as a backing should any foreign voice track be made in the future.

The final mixed track will be used as it stands for TV broadcast or video use. If the film is for theatrical release, it will have to be re-recorded from its magnetic form onto optical sound negative ready to form the sound stripe on combined (or "married") prints.

NEGATIVE CUTTING Throughout production, it is vital to log the key numbers from the edge of the film on each roll of rushes when they come in. These should be recorded scene by scene so that each piece of negative can be identified with its scene at neg cutting stage. The negative cutter is not interested in the action; his/her concern is with these edge numbers, which occur every 16 frames in 35mm and every 20 frames in 16mm. By reading the edge numbers wherever he finds a cut, the neg cutter can first identify the roll of negative in which the scene occurs and then see how many frames from the last edge number the cut has been made.

The cut negative is assembled in two rolls known as A and B rolls. The opticals marked on the cutting copy will also have been taken care of in preparing the negative. The completed A and B rolls, together with the cutting copy, are delivered to the laboratory ready for grading.

Sc 3

Sc 4

← A roll

Sc 1

Sc 2

← B roll

NEGATIVE CUTTING
A and B roll cutting avoids joins showing on the prints. At each cut, the negative is switched to the other roll and black space is inserted.

1

2

THE PRINTED STAGE
The rush prints which you have edited to make the cutting copy will have been made at different times and are likely to have varying appearance even when derived from one roll or batch of negative.

Many things can be wrong with a print, even if the negative is perfect. 1 is an example of a too heavy print, while 2 is too light.

The faults here are of color bias. Number 3 has been graded too blue, 4 too pink and 5 too yellow.

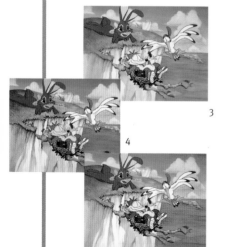

3

4

5

6 shows the frames of gray scale and color card which are shot at the head of all rostrum rolls. They indicate print density (gray scale) and color bias. Number 7 shows a corrected color grading.

COLOR GRADING AND FINAL PRINTING The rolls of rush print from which the cutting copy is assembled may vary considerably in color quality. It is a good idea to go through the cutting copy with the graders in the laboratory to tell them where there is a scene which is particularly good or bad. Also you may need to explain your intentions. For example, something you may have meant to be a subtle pale blue background can look to a grader like a white that needs correction. If there seem to be serious problems of over- or under-exposure, referring to the negative will show whether the scene is correctable. (Usually, of course, such a problem would be noticed at rush print stage and the negative checked then.) The first print made from the A and B rolls is unlikely to be absolutely correct. Laboratories are usually prepared to make more than one attempt at the grading and charge for only one trial print. If you ask for additional correction after that, delicate negotiation as to how the next print is charged may be necessary!

The final corrected print will be mute if it is for television or video, and transferred to tape with the original magnetic sound. For theatrical release, a combined print with the optical soundtrack alongside the picture will be made.

If several prints are to be made, it is customary to make a duplicate negative immediately and put away the original A and B rolls as a safety master. The dupe negative is used for printing the copies. If it gets damaged or worn, the original is available for making more dupes.

Soundtracks and sound mixing are now commonly made up on digital systems. The picture cutting copy is transferred to time-coded videotape. The time code is linked to the controlling code in the digital sound system and maintains the synchronization of sound and picture. Instead of measuring in feet, though, the video time code is in hours, minutes, seconds, and then frames. The

6

7

Sound Cue Sheet		Production RED RIDING HOOD				Sheet no. ONE			
Track No.									
Action Cues	Footage	1 VOICE(1) DIALOG	2 VOICE(2) NARRATION	3 FX1 FOOTSTEPS	4 FX2	5 FX3	6 MUSIC	7	8	9
ON LEADER ZERO	12									
SYNC PLOP	9									
START FADE IN EXTERIOR COTTAGE	12									
	15				OPEN AIR ATMOSPHERE	EXTRA BIRDSONG	MUSIC (1)			
	20		NARRATOR EARLY ONE MORNING...	..STEPS (MOTHER)						
	23	MOTHER	THE SET OFF							
	25	NOW MY DAUGHTER								
	30	...CAREFUL								
DISSOLVE TO WOOD	35			R.R.H. STEPS						
	40									
	45									
	50									

MIXING SOUNDTRACKS ON FILM
The picture cutting copy and all the component sound tracks, now completely edited and synched, are taken with a dubbing chart to the sound room. Here the picture and all the sound tracks are run on machines electronically interlocked to maintain sync during the mixing session.

◄ On the dubbing chart, the precise footage from the frontt of the film at which each sound or area of sound begins and ends is marked. If necessary, guidance is added as to the loudness or softness desired, and fade-ins and cross-fades are marked. The mixer works chiefly to a footage counter, but picture cues are noted as an extra guide. It is common to premixs elements like the sound effects to simplify the process.

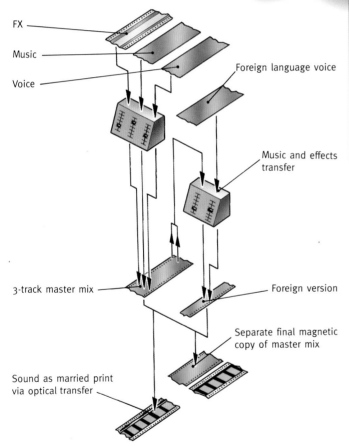

FX

Music

Voice

Foreign language voice

Music and effects transfer

3-track master mix

Foreign version

Separate final magnetic copy of master mix

Sound as married print via optical transfer

▲ At the final stage, the elements of voice, music, and sound effects are balanced and recorded on a single strand of film which carries three tracks. This is the three track magnetic master mix. It can be either mono or stereo. A back-up transfer, of the music effects only, is made for possible use with a foreign (or different) voice track.

recorder stores the sounds on hard disk and has a visual display showing where each sound is placed in relation to the picture. As with film dubbing, the sounds are assembled in separate strands so that they can be treated individually at the mixing stage. Digital systems contain a large number of separate channels or "tracks" so that there is ample room to store all the sounds you need. Sounds can be loaded in from any source, either magnetic film, or all kinds of recording tape, or from stored effects in the library which normally accompanies such systems. The sounds can be moved up and down at will, played back and reviewed until a satisfactory sync is achieved. One of the advantages of such systems is that sounds can be lengthened or shortened without changing their pitch. This is important for animation because effects usually need to be shorter and sharper than they are for live action. Once all the sound—music, dialogue, and effects—has been loaded into the system, the channels can be mixed to get a final mono or stereo mix to be transferred either to videotape or to magnetic film.

Digital editing is also now common for picture assembly. The uncut negative rolls are loaded onto disk with their key numbers used to identify them. They can then be edited as video. Various combinations can be tried without having to touch the original film. When a satisfactory edited version is complete, the digital print system prints out the key numbers in the correct order, and the negative is cut accordingly.

In more technically advanced studios, the animation picture may not have been shot as film, but recorded and then edited on disk. In that case, it needs no further treatment before going to the sound-laying stage.

Preparing Credits

It is always best to keep credits to a minimum, but sometimes they have to be extensive. In some countries, industry regulations require that everyone's name down to the last trainee must be included.

Broadly, the customary credits are for directors; producer (and sometimes executive producer); composer; lighting camera (for model films); rostrum camera; editors; sound editor (if different); animation director; key animators; background designer. All the other assistants, trainees, and gofers can be named, but only if compelled by rule or convenience. Voice artists, too, are frequently credited, particularly if they are famous performers.

Customarily, all technical credits come at the end of the film or program, and only the main title at the beginning, with possibly, "a film by . . ." if it is a near solo effort by a known name.

If the film has been commissioned or financed by a sponsor or a group of sponsors, they are usually named in a form of words like "produced by (company name) for CBS Television, Time-Life, NHK Japan, etc." There are also various combinations of "in association with" or "a CBS production." Most broadcasting organizations have definite rules about such wording, depending on the degree of their involvement in the production.

Because all their effort has gone into the animation of a film, animators rarely seem to put elaborate graphics and movement into their title sequences and credit titles. They tend to be plain and practical in making a frame for the film itself. Feature film and television program makers, on the other hand, are often keen on a bit of decorative animation or graphics to embellish their productions.

Animated title sequences of between half a minute and one and a half minutes are frequently commissioned from animation studios or graphic designers working with animation studios.

TECHNICAL REQUIREMENTS Here the main criteria are legibility and framing. The accompanying diagram gives the limits for the placing of lettering. In addition, a graticule or field chart is invaluable when designing credits. Not only does it give you a grid on which you can plan your screen limits, but it also supplies horizontal and vertical lines as useful guides for aligning the type. It is best to use

SAFETY AREA FOR TITLES The outer line of the diagram shows the limits of the Academy frame. The inner working is an estimate of television cut off. The rectangle with the cross shows you the safe limits for television titles.

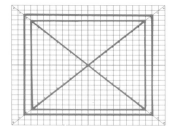

CREDITS FOR A SHORT FILM Credits from an 8-minute film commissioned from a solo animator. The name of the film alone comes at the beginning. For short films like this, only those directly involved are named.

CREDITS ON A LONGER FEATURE FILM
Very often the voice artists on these films are famous names which will help to sell the film, so they are given credits at the beginning with the main title. All the other production credits come at the end.

clear typefaces or boldly hand-drawn letters for the titling. Over-complex or spindly letters are hard to read, particularly when credit titles move along at a great speed. Plain backgrounds are always best, and if you are going to use colored letters instead of black and white, they should always be on a plain, strongly contrasting color. Colored lettering on a complex pattern or a photographic background is always a problem to read.

CHOOSING COLORS
For legibility, the lettering color should contrast sharply with the background. The tones as well as the color should contrast. White or bright lettering obviously should be chosen for a dark background and black, or dark against light.

The Farm

with the voices of:
Richard Burton
The Pig

Audrey Hepburn
The Cow

Marilyn Monroe
Mrs.Chicken

Script and story by
William Wordsworth

Music
Gustav Holst

Lyrics of the songs
Richard Rogers

Animation Directors
Long John Silver
Charlie Chaplin

Key Animators
Jim Hawkins
Arthur Benbow
Alan Breck Stewart
Charles Edward Stuart
Rob Roy McGregor
Marie de Guise

Animators
Name One	Name Two
Name Three	Name Four
Name Five	Name Six
Name Seven	Name Eight
Name Nine	Name Ten
Name Eleven	Name Twelve

Assistants
Name One	Name Two
Name Three	Name Four
Name Five	Name Six
Name Seven	Name Eight
Name Nine	Name Ten
Name Eleven	Name Twelve
Name Thirteen	Name Fouteen
Name Fifteen	Name Sixteen
Name Seventeen	Name Eighteen
Name Nineteen	Name Twenty

Background Designer
Giorgio Vasari

Background Artists
Piero della Francesca
Lucrezia Borgia
Lorenzo Ghiberti

▲ Where there is a long list of names it will probably be put on a "roller title," where the names pass vertically up through the screen. The other credits are on separate cards which dissolve one into the other.

Camera
Slow and Unreliable Rostrum Co.

Editor
Edward Scissorhands

Sound Mixed at
The Deaf Studio

Production Co-ordinator
Maria Martin

Producer
Harold Wilson

Directed by
Franz von Bismarck

A Loose Leaf Production
(Loose Leaf logo)
in association with
FOX TELEVISION
(Logo)

MCMLXXXVLL © LOOSE LEAF PRODUCTIONS

Counter changing lettering to accentuate a background with both dark and light areas may leave an optical puzzle.

Budgets: Drawn Animation

The largest cost in animation is labor, which is related to time—the number of working hours, days, or weeks—as well as the fees you pay yourself or others.

Budgeting and a production schedule are thus closely related. Even if you are working entirely to please yourself, you should make some kind of plan of how much work you can complete in a specified time, and if you are taking someone else's money to finance your work, a planned schedule and a budget are essential.

EMPLOYMENT AND OVERHEADS COSTS Even if you are self-employed and working alone, you will need to put a realistic price on your time which covers all your costs. Don't forget that this should provide a margin to cover tax and insurance, vacation time, illness, or other periods when you are not working.

When hiring others to work with you, it is important to be clear from the beginning what rate of pay you will give and what return you expect. In some cases, payment is made per foot of animation rather than for time. It is easier to calculate a footage rate for animators and assistant animators than for cel workers, who are more often paid on a time basis. Cost per foot is a sum calculated to pay for all the drawing required for 16 film frames of animation.

This again illustrates the relationship between time and cost. Your animator's footage rate has to be assessed against both your available money and how many feet per week are set as a target. Without that target, any production schedule will fall to pieces, and the ancillary costs of those paid on a time basis will also be affected. A shortfall of footage output per week means either that you will be paying for idle time for your cel workers or for overtime as the schedule runs past the deadline.

Rostrum camera rental, recording and sound-mixing facilities, laboratory processing, and digital post production are

Further Information

Rostrum camerawork, p.26
Cel, p.52

SMALL UNIT BUDGET

This is a budget prepared for an eight-minute TV film, *The Mill*, made by an animator/designer working alone. She painted on glass directly under the camera, so there were no labor costs apart from her own, but the time spent on the camera was proportionately higher. A deal was struck with a rostrum company to allow her to work continuously at a reduced weekly charge. Production management was handled by an established production company for a separate production fee. Overall production schedule was 22 weeks.

	% of Total Costs
Direct costs:	
Storyboard and trial sequences to gain commission	10.98%
Animator/director	32.22%
Production accounting (intermittent)	0.59%
Cameraman (occasional assistance)	2.20%
Salary overheads (tax & insurance)	1.35%
Materials (art)	1.83%
Film and tape stock	2.84%
Post production (pic & sound includes processing to final print, also editor and sound editing)	16.87%
Rostrum camera time	19.22%
Music: composing and performing	5.49%
Travel and transportation	0.37%
Miscellaneous costs	0.92%
Insurance and legal	1.82%
Production overheads (proportion of studio overheads)	3.30%
	100.00%

BUDGETS
Budgeting for production is subject to so many variables that it is difficult to present a generally applicable example.

E

Fil

Labo

Video

COST HEADINGS

Here is a fairly comprehensive list of the cost headings for a standard cel-animation production. These are what is known as direct costs; overheads, producer fee, and profit form a separate calculation.

Labor

Producer
Animation director
Layout artist
Key animators
Assistant animators
In-betweeners
Background designer
Background artist
*Renderers
*Tracers
*Painters (also called colorists)
*If own camera: rostrum operator and allowance for camera time at hourly rate
*If outside rostrum facility used: hourly rate for both camera and operator
Paper, cel, poster board, paint, pens, pencils, markers, inks
Voice artists
Musician (composer)
Musicians (performers)
Sound studio rental (voice)
Sound studio rental (music)
Sound effects (library)
Sound effects (homemade)
Sound studio (effects)
Tape stock
Transfer charge (from ¼-inch tape or DAT to film or videotape)
Final mixing of sound tracks
Editor
Assistant editor
Cutting room rental (if necessary)
Magnetic sound stock
*Picture negative
*Sound stock, black and white (if married print)
*Negative developing and rush prints
*Negative cutting
*Sound transfer to optical negative (for married print)
*Answer print (first trial print)
*Show print
*...pes for line-testing
*...be transfer of final show print
*...nsfer time and tape copies)

Cel workers

...amera costs

...erials

all costed on a time basis—so much per hour or day—or in the case of laboratory work, at so much per foot. Standard rates can be ascertained, and often special deals negotiated, but you must be accurate in your estimate of the time needed in each facility.

For a solo filmmaker, the overheads are mainly premises and equipment. If you work in one room, overheads are the rent and upkeep of the room, insurance, light, heat, telephone, correspondence, and so on. As soon as you employ other people, the situation becomes more complex. You will need more space, so rent and taxes on premises will escalate rapidly, and you will have to pay for taxes, liability insurance, the provision of health and safety facilities, and basic equipment such as desks and chairs. If you buy technical equipment, you should cost the purchase price in the overhead figure and calculate the replacement cost on a sum per year against the estimated life of the equipment. This sum, called depreciation, needs to be included with all the other studio overheads to make an annual overhead figure. Proportionate to the time scheduled for any production, a part of the annual overhead can be assigned to the production overhead figure. Systems of budgeting vary, depending on the purpose of the animation, but as a rule it is customary to work out the direct costs for any production and then calculate a producer or production fee as a percentage mark-up on that figure. This percentage also includes the profit margin.

COST OVERRUNS As mentioned earlier, the overruns on time are the most common reasons for going over budget, because they relate directly to the cost of labor. Increases in overheads (steep rises in rent, for example) or in technical costs (a special technique requiring expensive laboratory work) can usually be budgeted for ahead of the production, but with an overrun on animating time, you will have to pay more for labor than estimated, and other aspects will also be made more expensive. A director's indecision, requiring the reworking of scenes, is another source of unforeseen expense; if you wish to have the luxury of second thoughts, you must allow for them in an increased budget.

◀ Asterisked items will be unnecessary if digital equipment is used to color the finished animation and it is not shot on film but recorded onto disk. However, the cost of transferring the complete work from disk to either film or broadcast videotape will have to be substituted.

Budgets: Computer Animation

The extent to which computers enter the production process varies widely from studio to studio and filmmaker to filmmaker, so it is hard to make a universal rule about costing computer animation.

If we assume, however, a production in which all the things traditionally used in animation drawing—tracing, coloring, filming, and final picture master—are done digitally, we would arrive at percentages of production costs that indicate that real computer costs amount to about 60 percent of direct costs excluding overheads and profit.

When studios take storyboard and preliminary work to an outside facility house for the digital processes, they are charged a rate per hour for the machine time and operator. Although such rates are fixed, it is often possible to negotiate an overall deal at a lower rate if the work is going to be prolonged.

If a studio uses its own machine, it is normal practice to put into the budget a time cost comparable to the current price of outside facilities.

It seems generally accepted that if you estimate a job which will allow you to buy the computer and software to produce it, it is advisable to add 50% to your initial estimate of the cost of these items. Experience has shown that additional equipment and programs beyond your initial projection are frequently needed, as well as servicing and repairs. These costs will add half as much again to the basic computer prices.

COSTS OF A COMPUTER ANIMATION PRODUCTION EXPRESSED IN PERCENTAGES	
Studio overheads	30%
Initial work on storyboard, sound track, and design (also include final sound mixing)	30%
Computer time and operators	40%
TOTAL	100%

This illustration from *Crumble* by Ruth Lingford is from a sequence drawn directly on an ordinary Apple Macintosh. It was then transferred frame by frame to videotape. Because the equipment is relatively simple, the process is correspondingly slow.

Budgets: Model Animation

In general, the costs of model animation are similar to those of drawn animation, with the largest item being artists' and technicians' paid time.

The difference between the two forms lies in the fact that, for drawn animation, the bulk of the time is consumed in preparing the artwork for camera; the shooting time is relatively short and foreseeable. With model work, on the other hand, the time spent making the models is controllable, but the animating time may be extended by unforeseen problems during the shooting.

Here are some general comments about budgeting for model work on a commercial scale. The preproduction stages—script, storyboarding, and voice recording—are the same as for drawn work, as are office costs and post-production. Model work needs fewer animators, but more specialist technicians for making models, costumes, and sets. The position of director of photography is important and highly paid, and he or she will have assistants. A carpenter is also essential for set and stage building.

STUDIO FACILITIES Puppet production needs more square feet of space than drawn work; a 3-D studio must have at least one large clear room with reasonable ceiling height. A typical studio would contain a main office, editing room, costume room, kitchen, model-making workshop, and shooting studio. There should be room for at least two shooting stages. While animation is being shot on one, the other is being prepared and lit so that there is no break in the filming. If the pressure of work means that two or more animators are shooting, then the number of stages will increase.

SET CONSTRUCTION AND PUPPET MAKING Some of the materials required for the sets may be expensive, though wages are the principal expense. It is sometimes necessary to build duplicate sets to speed up the shooting by working on two stages at once.

The puppet-making part of production is often put out to subcontractors who specialize in such work. Unless there is a perpetual rolling programme of different productions requiring different puppets, a permanent staff might have periods of idleness.

COSTS OF A MODEL ANIMATION PRODUCTION EXPRESSED IN PERCENTAGES

Preproduction	1.5%
Production personnel (wages)	49.0%
Studio facility	15.7%
Voice recordings	3.1%
Art dept., model building, sets, costumes	2.3%
Puppet building	7.6%
Camera dept.	5.0%
Stills photography (animation dept.)	0.8%
Picture and sound editing	2.1%
Sound mixing	2.3%
Music	4.4%
Lab, video, delivery	6.2%
TOTAL	**100%**

The studio which supplied these percentages has not included the cost of cameras, lights, etc., since they were already fully equipped. The production in question was a musical one, so the music budget is relatively high.

CAMERA AND LIGHTING On a professional scale, a large capital investment is required for this equipment. A secondhand stop-frame 16mm camera can be acquired for a few hundred dollars, but a professional standard 35mm camera will cost many thousand, and broadcast-quality video cameras with stop-frame recording facilities, either onto tape or digitally, will be thousands more. The remaining items—lights, tripods and geared heads, scaffolding, and "magic arms" to hold lights and models—will also cost a considerable sum, and there are maintenance expenses.

For high-budget work on commercials and features, computer-based motion-control rigs are used, another large expense. Much of the equipment, of course, can be rented as it is needed, but this will add considerably to the cost of the production, so for large productions or long series, it is more economical to purchase.

LABORATORY PROCESSING Unless you can negotiate a waiver of the customary minimum footage charge, the cost of processing the short lengths typical of model shooting will be high. This cost, however, is not going to be as large as that of finding a fault in the filming after weeks of animation. It is therefore good practice to put material into the labs as often as possible.

Presentation

Now is the time when you must convince people of what you can do —but before you've done it.

How you present your work depends on your aims. You may be trying to sign up for a course or get hired as a studio trainee. Or you may have animation experience, and be trying to secure funding for a project or commission. Let us suppose that, with no previous experience, you are going to approach either a possible employer or college course. You have little or no completed animated work, but enthusiasm and an obvious devotion to animation. What can you present to persuade either of them to take you on?

For drawing work, it is not enough to produce neat copies of well-known characters from past or current cartoon films. What your prospective employer or teacher is looking for is an ability to draw a figure from every aspect. If you can, create characters of your own, and draw them in different poses from a variety of viewpoints. It is an advantage to have some figure drawings to show. Neatness and cleanliness of presentation are important—no employer wants a messy employee, no matter what his or her potential brilliance may be. For model animation it is desirable to show ability not only to make pleasing figures and models on a small scale, but also to have a flair for the mechanical and engineering side of frame-by-frame work. For model and drawn animation, show a grasp of story construction by putting together a storyboard.

Sometimes it is possible to judge an applicant's potential from his or her attitude to sound. To have put together a short sound piece on your home tape recorder is a way of demonstrating what you can do. Above all, make your presentation a selection of the best you can do rather than offering a quantity of stuff in the hope that something among it may catch the eye.

NO PROFESSIONAL EXPERIENCE, BUT SOME ANIMATION TO SHOW
The fact that you have something on film or video is an indication that you are resourceful enough to find your way to equipment, or technically skilled enough to construct your own. As with the material in a drawn portfolio, make sure that the film or video represents your best work. Including everything you have done, some of which may be poorly lit, out of focus, or repetitive, will only try the patience of those you hope to impress. Sketchbooks, designs, and storyboards used as supporting material should also be selected with care. Brief pieces of animation of high quality will give the viewer the idea that there is more of the same in prospect. The same material mixed in with a mass of mediocre stuff does not allow that estimate to be made. While a potential employer will look more for technical competence, both employers and course directors will look for the power to communicate.

FORMAT Standard home-use videotape is the most universally useful form in which to show your material. 16mm or 35mm film are also viable, but 8mm can present problems. If you are showing computer work, it is probably better to have it transferred to videotape because of the possible incompatibility of different systems. Your disk may not play on their machines.

PRESENTING FOR A COMMISSION Funding bodies or broadcasting companies expect to receive proposals in a package which includes a storyboard; a sample of the design of the characters and background; a written script; a recording of the soundtrack or some clear indication of its character; and, if possible, a short pilot sequence of completed animation.

They also need a detailed budget and evidence that you either have or can gain access to the technical resources necessary to complete the piece. If the project is a pilot for a series, you will also have to present outlines of at least ten more episodes to show that the idea can support a series.

STORYBOARD The storyboard should be intelligible without explanation. The drawing can be quite sketchy, provided you can give a clear presentation of the finished style with a piece of finished artwork. If possible, you should try to present your storyboard in person. You have the clearest idea of the flow of the piece, and, by acting it out in something like the real time of the film, you can carry it through. Leaving other people to plow through a storyboard at careful reading speed is damaging to its effect.

Funding institutions and broadcasters vary in their methods. In some cases, you may have only to convince one person. In others, you may be dealing with a committee. There is one organization connected to the promotion of animation which requires applicants for funding to provide 80 copies in two languages of the full package described above!

SOUNDTRACK To record a soundtrack somewhere close to the finished one may be impractical or too expensive. A rough one, known as a "scratch track," should aim to be as lively as possible with some attempt at voice characterization and music for the style which you intend. You can, for these purposes, use copyright

Further Information
☞
Storyboards, p.16

PRESENTATION KIT
Here are the basic elements to present for a possible project: character drawings, a script and a pilot sequence of animation on videotape, preferably with sound.

commercial recordings, but be sure that the commissioned music it represents is possible within your resources.

PACKAGING The complete presentation of storyboard, script, artwork, sound, and pilot videotape should be easy to look at and pleasant to handle. An envelope full of disorganized pieces of paper will not show up very well. Bind the storyboard and script in loose-leaf notebooks so that the sheets can be opened up and displayed side by side if necessary. Mark every item—indeed every page—with the project title and your own name, address, and telephone number.

SECURING A CONTRACT An offer of funding will bring with it some form of written agreement or contract. This will define in detail what you are expected to supply and what the funders will give in return—and when they will give it. Most established broadcasters and known funding institutions have standard procedures which are easy to check. In return for full funding, you will probably be

expected to resign most distribution rights, but you should expect to receive additional payments for extra transmissions, sales as videos, or international distribution. In most cases, the payments will be affected by deductions for the distributors' or funders' expenses.

With smaller and less well-known sources of funding, be particularly careful that you retain adequate control over your material. It has been known for filmmakers to find that, in getting funding for a project, they have signed away the right to use the characters created for that project in any further work of their own.

There are also dangers in committing yourself on ill-defined promises of funds. Before you incur heavy expenses—even an overdraft—you must be clear that there will be definite stages of payment in a signed agreement. It is always advisable to ask for a substantial initial payment before work starts.

Index

Page numbers in *italics* refer to illustrations

Credits

Many topics in this book would have been impossible to cover without the assistance of the following:

On various aspects of model animation production the author is indebted chiefly to David Johnson of Famous Flying Films for his knowledge and advice. The demonstrations of puppet-making and set construction were the work of Beverley Knowlden, and Cathy Greenhalgh supplied invaluable information on lighting. Andy Stavely of 3 Peach Animation also made a helpful contribution.
Much of the article on computer work was supplied by Stephen Weston of Whitehorse Films together with his partner Lisa Beattie. Ruth Lingford, also, was kind enough to give a description of her working method. The author was also able to consult Jerry Hibbert of Hibbert Ralph, and Jill Thomas of Richard Purdum Productions on their approach to the use of computers in the production of commercials.

Quarto would like to thank all the animators and animation companies who have so kindly contributed examples of their work for publication in this book.

We would also like to thank the following for permission to reproduce images (Key: *a* above, *b* below, *l* left, *r* right):

Cambridge Animation Systems **55**; Joel Finler **6a** & **b**, **35b**, **47br**, **98** & **110**, **104/105**, **112a**, **113r**, **136r**, **139**, **145**, **152a** & **b**, **154a**; Halas & Batchelor **31al**, **34–5**, **108a**; National Film Board of Canada **8b**, **108b**, **123b**, **128b**; Raytech BBS **70**, **124**.

Additional acknowledgements: **8** software used on Metadata created by Francis Lazarus and Anne Verroust; **17** Cleo Harrington's storyboard comes from the film *Grow Up!*; **19a** & **81a** commercial produced by Heye & Partner GmbH, animated by 3 Peach; **19b** & **134a** commercial produced by Bartle Bogle Hegarty Ltd for Levi Strauss & Co, animated by Aaargh! Animation; **42–53** drawings from a campaign for Cadbury's Caramel, by Mike Adams and Ginger Gibbons; **57** *The Legends of Treasure Island* © Central Broadcasting Ltd; **58** cut-outs are from *The Glass Ceiling* by Leeds Animation Workshop; **71** *Coiled Gold Mutation* comes from Organic Television, commissioned by Manchester City Art Galleries; **72–75** examples of computer animation by Stephen Weston, at Whitehorse Films; **112b** © Manga Entertainment Ltd; **126** commercial produced by Collett Dickenson Pearce for Gaymers; **132** commercial produced by J Walter Thompson, London, for Nestlé; **135** commercial produced for Public Broadcasting Corporation, USA, sponsored by Mobil Oil; **134b** commercial produced by Ogilvy & Mather Ltd, computer animation by 601 FX; **134r** Commercial produced by J Walter Thompson, USA, for Warner-Lambert Corporation, © Pixar 1994; **135bl** 'Coca-Cola', 'Coke' and 'Fanta' are registered trade marks of The Coca-Cola Company. This image is reproduced with kind permission from The Coca-Cola Company. **135br** commercial produced by Ogilvy & Mather for NRG Lucozade, effects director Christian Hogue; **137** commercial produced by Walsh Trott Chick Smith; **138b** commercial produced by Grey Advertising Ltd; **138al** commercial produced by Abbott Mead Vickers-BBDO Ltd; **138ar** commercial produced by J Walter Thompson, New York, for Mott's USA; **140a** commercial produced by J Walter Thompson, London, for Nestlé; **140bl** commercial produced by Leo Burnett, Chicago, for Kellogg's; **140br** & **141r**

commercials produced by Bozell Inc, USA, for Merrill Lynch; **140a** commercial produced by Humphreys Bull & Barker for Rotary; **148–9**: *Astrofarm* © Andy Ellis/Filmfair Ltd 1991; *The Wombles* © Elizabeth Beresford/Filmfair Ltd; *White Bear's Secret* © Filmfair/L'Ecole de Loisirs; *The Legends of Treasure Island* © Central Broadcasting Ltd; *Shoe People* © James Driscoll 1990; **158–9** illustrations from Mike Adams and Ginger Gibbons' commercial for Cadbury's Caramel, produced by Geoff Dunbar.

Demonstration photography is the copyright of Quarto Inc.

The technique of sand animation was demonstrated by Michelle Smith on equipment made by Jeremy Moorshead of the Royal College of Art. The flicker drawings on the page corners are the work of Ronaldo Canfora.

Our thanks to Chromacolour, London, for supplying some of the tools and equipment used in photography.

Finally, special thanks to Mike Adams and Ginger Gibbons, formerly of Grand Slamm, for their considerable co-operation in providing some of the illustrative material used in the section on drawn animation; to Aaargh! Animation for their interest in and contribution to this project; and to Pat Raine Webb at ASIFA, UK for her kind help with picture research.

Every effort has been made to acknowledge copyright holders and Quarto would like to apologise if any omissions have been made.